THE FIRST WORLD WAR

CONTEXT AND COMMENTARY

Series Editor: ARTHUR POLLARD

THE FIRST WORLD WAR

Dominic Hibberd

MACMILLAN

First published 1990

Published by
MACMILLAN EDUCATION LTD
Houndmills, Basingstoke, Hampshire RG21 2XS
and London
Companies and representatives
throughout the world

Typeset by Wessex Typesetters
(Division of The Eastern Press Ltd)
Frome, Somerset

Printed in Hong Kong

British Library Cataloguing in Publication Data
The First World War.
1. English Literature, 1900–1945 – Anthologies
I. Hibberd, Dominic
820.800912
ISBN 0–333–39776–2
ISBN 0–333–39777–0 pbk

Contents

List of Plates

1. *Injured Innocence* by Bernard Partridge, *Punch* (31 May 1916) page 361. The German Ogre stands on the torn 'scrap of paper', the treaty which had guaranteed Belgian neutrality. Behind him is Bernhardi's slogan, 'Weltmacht oder Niedergang' ('World-power or downfall').
   Photograph © Bodleian Library, from *N. 2706 d 10*.

2. *The Merry-Go-Round* by Mark Gertler (1916). '. . . in this combination of blaze, and violent and mechanised rotation and complete involution, utterly mindless intensity of sensational extremity, you have made a real and ultimate revelation' (D. H. Lawrence to Gertler, 9 October 1916).
   Photograph © Tate Gallery.

3. *The Signing of the Peace in the Hall of Mirrors, 28 June 1919* by William Orpen. In front of the leaders of the victorious countries, German representatives sign the Treaty of Versailles. The overwhelming architecture and crooked mirrors make a mocking background. One of the reflected silhouettes is Orpen himself, official British artist at the conference.
   Photograph © The Trustees of the Imperial War Museum.

4. *The Menin Road 1918* by Adrian Hill. British troops pass through the site of the old town gate in the walls of Ypres. Plates 4 and 5 were published together as No 1 in a series 'Ten Years After 1918–1928' in *Answers Magazine* (20 October 1928).
   Photograph © Bodleian Library, from *John Johnson Collection: Great War. Box 24*.

5. *The Menin Gate 1928* by Adrian Hill. The new gate, completed in 1927, is a memorial to the armies of the

British Empire who held the Ypres Salient; it bears the
names of 54 889 soldiers who have no known graves.
Photograph © Bodleian Library, from *John Johnson
Collection* as above.

Acknowledgements

The author and publishers wish to thank the following who have kindly given permission for the use of copyright material: Carcanet Press Ltd. for extracts from *War Letters* by Ivor Gurney, 1983; Chatto and Windus, The Hogarth Press on behalf of the Estate of Wilfred Owen for 'Dulce et Decorum Est' by Wilfred Owen from *The Complete Poems and Fragments* ed. J. Stallworthy, The Hogarth Press, 1983; and on behalf of the Executors of the H. G. Wells Estate for extracts from *Mr Britling Sees it Through* by H. G. Wells, Chatto and Windus; Curtis Brown Group Ltd on behalf of the Estate of Sir Winston Churchill for extracts by Winston S. Churchill from *Sunday Pictorial*, 20 May 1917. Copyright © the Estate of Sir Winston Churchill; Faber and Faber Ltd for an extract from *In Parenthesis* by David Jones, 1937; William Heinemann Ltd for material from *The Middle Parts of Fortune* by Frederick Manning, Peter Davies, 1977; David Higham Associates Ltd for an extract from 'Meditation of the Waking English Officer' from *The End of the War* by Herbert Read, Faber and Faber, 1933; Macmillan, London and Basingstoke, with Cambridge University Press, Inc. for material from *The Economic Consequences of the Peace* by J. M. Keynes, 1919; and with Michael Gibson for 'Breakfast' by W. W. Gibson, *The Nation*, 17 October 1914; Macmillan Publishing Company for 'Sisteen Dead Men' from *The Poems of W. B. Yeats* ed. Richard J. Finneran. Copyright © 1924 by Macmillan Publishing Company, renewed 1952 by Bertha Georgie Yeats; John Murray (Publishers) Ltd for extracts from *Poor Bloody Infantry* by Bernard Martin, 1987; Peters Fraser and Dunlop for extracts from 'Third Ypres' from *Poems of Many Years* by Edmund Blunden, William Collins Sons and Co. Ltd; Pillans and Wilson Ltd for an extract from *The Wine Press: A Tale of War* by Alfred Noyes, William Blackwood and Sons, 1913; The Bertrand Russell Estate for an extract from *The Labour Leader*, 10 September 1914;

George T. Sassoon for Siegfried Sassoon's public protest, 1917 and an extract from *Memoirs of an Infantry Officer* by Siegfried Sassoon; with Viking Penguin, Inc. for 'The Rear Guard', 'Does it Matter?' and 'Passing the New Menin Gate' from *The Collected Poems* by Siegfried Sassoon. Copyright © 1918/1920 by E. P. Dutton and Co., Inc. 1936, 1946, 1947, 1948 by Siegfried Sassoon; Sidgewick and Jackson Ltd for 'The Volunteer' from *The Volunteer and Other Poems* by Herbert Asquith, 1916; Timothy d'Arch Smith for an extract from 'The Answer' from *Poetical Works* by Gilbert Frankau, Chatto and Windus, 1923; The Society of Authors with Mrs Nicolete Gray on behalf of the Laurence Binyon Estate for 'The Test' by Laurence Binyon; and on behalf of The Bernard Shaw Estate for an extract from *Common Sense About the War* by Bernard Shaw, 1930; The Estate of H. M. Tomlinson for an extract from *All Our Yesterdays* by H. M. Tomlinson, William Heinemann, 1930; Unwin Hyman Ltd for material from *Principles of Social Reconstruction* by Bertrand Russell; and a letter from A. G. West, in *Autobiography* Volume II by Bertrand Russell, 1968; and 'Two Years After' from *A Ballad of Four Brothers* by George Willis, 1921; A. P. Watt Ltd on behalf of the Literary Executors of the Estate of H. G. Wells for material from *In the Fourth Year* by H. G. Wells and 'Why Britain Went to War' from *The War That Will End War* by H. G. Wells. Every effort has been made to trace all copyright holders, but if any have been inadvertently overlooked the publishers will be pleased to make the necessary arrangement at the first opportunity.

For my Father

Editor's Preface

J. H. Plumb has said that 'the aim of (the historian) is to understand men both as individuals and in their social relationships in time. "Social" embraces all of man's activities – economic, religious, political, artistic, legal, military, scientific – everything, indeed, that affects the life of mankind.' Literature is itself similarly comprehensive. From Terence onwards writers have embraced his dictum that all things human are their concern.

It is the aim of this series to trace the interweavings of history and literature, to show by judicious quotation and commentary how those actually working within the various fields of human activity influenced and were influenced by those who were writing the novels, poems and plays within the several periods. An attempt has been made to show the special contribution that such writers make to the understanding of their times by virtue of their peculiar imaginative 'feel' for their subjects and the intensely personal angle from which they observe the historical phenomena that provide their inspiration and come within their creative vision. In its turn the historical evidence, besides and beyond its intrinsic importance, serves to 'place' the imaginative testimony of the writers.

The authors of the several volumes in this series have sought to intermingle history and literature in the conviction that the study of each is enhanced thereby. They have been free to adopt their own approach within the broad general pattern of the series. The topics themselves have sometimes also a particular slant and emphasis. Commentary, for instance, has had to be more detailed in some cases than in others. All the contributors to the series are at one, however, in the belief (at a time when some critics would not only divorce texts from their periods but even from their authors) that literature is the creation of actual men and women, actually living in an identifiable set of historical circumstances, themselves both the creatures and the creators of their times.

ARTHUR POLLARD

1 Introduction

By assembling passages from some of the many different documents of the Great War, this book attempts to give an indication, necessarily brief and selective, of the ways in which writing interacted with the events of the time. Creative writers do not merely 'respond' to circumstances; they tend to be in advance of general opinion and to play some part in shaping it, so that they may take on the role of prophet, teacher or interpreter. They foresee, warn, encourage, comment, satirise, denounce, celebrate, commemorate, record. Sometimes they remain aloof, but that was not easy in 1914–18; Wilfred Owen remarked in 1915 that Keats had 'remained absolutely indifferent to Waterloo and all that commotion', but Keats never had to face the intense moral challenge of the casualty lists and the recruiting posters. *Are YOU in this? Why aren't YOU in khaki? Step into your place. 'Be honest with yourself – be certain that your so-called reason is not a selfish excuse' – Lord Kitchener – ENLIST TODAY. Take up the Sword of Justice. Fight for Freedom with the Strength of Free Men. Come lad: slip across and help. Each recruit brings peace nearer. More men and still more men.* (There was even a quotation from the national poet, wrenched horribly out of context: *Stand not upon the order of your going, but go at once – Shakespeare Macbeth 3.4. – Enlist now.*) If Keats had been born a century later, he, too, might have served on the Western Front, where Owen and many other writers saw what Richard Aldington later described as 'the last achievements of civilized men'.

Front-line experience set soldiers apart, giving them a knowledge which they could never fully communicate, but it is a modern misconception to suppose that they all became protesters or that all civilians were bellicose patriots. Aldington, C. E. Montague, Siegfried Sassoon, Robert Graves, and the many other volunteers who have had such a lasting effect on posterity's view of the First World War, wrote their

1

memoirs in the twenties when the dismal realities of peace, already analysed with Bloomsbury irony by John Maynard Keynes in 1919, had supplanted the desperate hopes of war. During the war, most protest came from a small band of civilians, Bertrand Russell prominent among them. The literature of 1914–18 cannot be understood without an awareness that most British people, soldiers as much as civilians, were convinced throughout the four years that Germany had to be driven out of Belgium and that military victory was therefore essential.

This book traces a chronological pattern, and the chronological table at the end should be referred to. It was not wholly coincidence that the public adulation of Rupert Brooke began at the moment when the Germans first used poison gas, or that Sassoon's protest was made in the year of the Russian revolutions, or that Owen wrote 'Dulce et Decorum Est' while Passchendaele was at its worst. Isaac Rosenberg's 'Break of Day in the Trenches', written just before the Somme, is not only a protest but also an expression of the private soldier's ironic yet dogged courage in the front line. The harrowing letter from a subaltern which T. S. Eliot sent to *The Nation* in 1917 (p.100 below) demonstrates how vividly Eliot, a civilian, was conscious of trench conditions at a time when *The Waste Land* was beginning to take shape. D. H. Lawrence's 'The Prussian Officer' shows a characteristic British dislike of Germans in the immediately pre-war period and Rudyard Kipling's 'Mary Postgate' reflects the emergence of 'hate' in the spring of 1915. Lawrence's savage references to 'Bottomleyism' in *Kangaroo* lack their full force until one reads some of Horatio Bottomley's journalism; reading Bottomley also suggests what kind of newspaper writing it was that provoked the fury of Sassoon and Owen. Sassoon's 1917 protest shows the influence of Russell's 1916 essays, which in their turn were influenced by Lawrence; the value they could have for a disenchanted officer is illustrated by A. G. West's remarkable 1916 letter to Russell (p.121 below). Sassoon's poems are in the direct Georgian tradition which led from John Masefield and Brooke before 1914 to W. W. Gibson's sceptical war verse in 1914–15 and on, through Sassoon, to Owen's unique achievement in 1918. Over the whole period there seems to hang the elegiac despair of A. E. Housman and the ironic, pitying genius of Thomas Hardy, the first two poets quoted below and the two who had most influence on the younger generation; Hardy's work in the decade before 1914 seems prophetic, and it was from his *The Dynasts* that Keynes chose a quotation to describe the workings of fate at the peace conference in 1919.

There is no typical writer of the Great War; the literature which it produced was as vast and diverse as the colossal human effort which the war represented. Only a very little of that literature is still read today. Even among the seventy or so authors quoted in this book, there are names that will be unfamiliar to the modern reader; some of the quotations are well known, but others are reprinted here for the first time. If the quotations have anything in common, it may be a vigour and often an elegance of language, marks of a civilisation which was tougher and more admirable than we tend to imagine and which did not die completely, as was once thought, when the war ended. The literature of 1914–18 offers not only lessons for the modern writer and unexplored territory for the researcher but also many rewards for the general reader.

2 The Coming of the War

Omens

European civilisation in the nineteenth century was often fearful for the future. Despite the hopes and achievements of the age, Romanticism always dreamed of ruin. From Byron's little poem 'Darkness' (1816) to H. G. Wells's fantasy, *The Time Machine* (1895), there were prophecies of the end. Mary Shelley's *Frankenstein* (1818) warned that man himself with his new science might be the architect of his own destruction. By the close of the Victorian period developments in science, philosophy and economics seemed to point towards the collapse of the established order. Nietzsche announced that God was dead, man being merely one species in a universe which depended on struggle and violence for survival. Mysterious bombings and assassinations all over Europe foreshadowed revolutions to come. Literature shared in the prevailing pessimism, as is evident from the novels of Thomas Hardy and Joseph Conrad and the poetry of Swinburne, A. E. Housman and the Decadents.

War and disaster provided subject matter for many poems. Soldiers appear frequently in work by Housman, Kipling, G. M. Hopkins and others. In Housman's *A Shropshire Lad*, perhaps the most widely read book of poetry in the years leading up to 1914, the call of war is repeatedly heard, luring young men from the tedious idleness of peace.

> On the idle hill of summer,
> Sleepy with the flow of streams,
> Far I hear the steady drummer
> Drumming like a noise in dreams.
>
> Far and near and low and louder,
> On the roads of earth go by,
> Dear to friends and food for powder,
> Soldiers marching, all to die.

4

East and west on fields forgotten
   Bleach the bones of comrades slain,
Lovely lads and dead and rotten;
   None that go return again.

Far the calling bugles hollo,
   High the screaming fife replies,
Gay the files of scarlet follow:
   Woman bore me, I will rise.

      A. E. Housman, *A Shropshire Lad* (1896), xxxv.

There seemed to be some fatal power that drew men towards conflict. Hardy represented it as the Immanent Will in *The Dynasts* (1903–8), his epic-drama of the Napoleonic wars, and in 'The Convergence of the Twain' (1912), a poem about the loss of the *Titanic* which might seem to foreshadow the wreck of the proud but drifting states of Europe only two years later.

      In a solitude of the sea
      Deep from human vanity,
And the Pride of Life that planned her, stilly couches she.

      Steel chambers, late the pyres
      Of her salamandrine fires,
Cold currents thrid, and turn to rhythmic tidal lyres.

      Over the mirrors meant
      To glass the opulent
The sea-worm crawls – grotesque, slimed, dumb, indifferent.

      Jewels in joy designed
      To ravish the sensuous mind
Lie lightless, all their sparkles bleared and black and blind.

Dim moon-eyed fishes near
Gaze at the gilded gear
And query: 'What does this vaingloriousness down
here? . . .

Well: while was fashioning
This creature of cleaving wing,
The Immanent Will that stirs and urges everything

Prepared a sinister mate
For her – so gaily great –
A Shape of Ice, for the time far and dissociate.

And as the smart ship grew
In stature, grace, and hue,
In shadowy silent distance grew the Iceberg too.

Alien they seemed to be:
No mortal eye could see
The intimate welding of their later history.

Or sign that they were bent
By paths coincident
On being anon twin halves of one august event,

Till the Spinner of the Years
Said 'Now!' And each one hears,
And consummation comes, and jars two hemispheres.

Thomas Hardy, 'The Convergence of the Twain'
(first published 1912).

Certainly fate and human vanity seemed active in European politics. In 1871 the Prussian army had marched in triumph through Paris, and in the same Hall of Mirrors at Versailles where the Allies were to force humiliating peace terms on Germany in 1919, King Wilhelm of Prussia had been proclaimed Kaiser (Caesar, Emperor) of a newly united Germany. Under his grandson, Wilhelm II, who acceded in 1888, the fledgeling state became ever more stridently nationalist, asserting its right to colonies and military strength. Apprehensive and aching for revenge, France moved towards new allies, first Russia, and then Great Britain in the *Entente Cordiale* of 1904. These three countries were to be the principal 'Allies' of 1914–18 against the 'Central Powers' of Germany and Austria-Hungary. The *Entente* led to an understanding, never fully made public, that Britain would assist France if she were attacked. The 'secret diplomacy' of the years before 1914 was later often regarded as a cause of the war, partly because it left everyone uncertain as to what Britain and other countries would do if hostilities were to break out. In each country there were some people who called for disarmament and some who demanded stronger defences. Hopes for disarmament produced a series of fruitless peace conferences at The Hague; pressure for more military spending contributed to an arms race. Armers and disarmers alike often warned the public that war was a very real danger. Popular war novels in several countries reflected, and perhaps contributed to, the nationalisms, fears and illusions of the time, describing how the perfect race, victims of unprovoked aggression, would defeat the villains in a swift campaign. One of the many British examples was William Le Queux's *The Invasion of 1910* (1906), first published as a *Daily Mail* serial advertised by 'Prussian soldiers' parading down Oxford Street. Such stories insisted that Britain was being infiltrated by German spies and that national defences needed to be massively strengthened.

Germans Prophesying War

When British people condemned Germany for seeking wealth and territory, they overlooked the fact that she wanted what Britain already had, but they did have some grounds for anxiety. It seemed that Germany was ruled by a creed of military expansion, racial supremacy and intensive profession-alism, under a vain, dictatorial Emperor. German authors made strong claims for their country's *Kultur*, a term which foreigners found to mean not 'culture' but a system of absolute state power in which individuals had no choice but were assigned to specialised tasks (hence British pride in democracy, amateurism, sportsmanship and all-round education). Three writers in particular came to be seen as spokesmen for 'Prussianism' or 'Prussian militarism': Nietzsche, Treitschke and Bernhardi. Friedrich Nietzsche had proclaimed the coming of the Superman, the new humanity which would control its own fate by will and force. Victory would be to the Teutonic 'blonde beast', prime example of the survival of the fittest (hence innumerable references to Germany as 'the Beast' in British wartime literature). Nietzsche's mouthpiece, the prophet Zarathustra, declares the values of the future and warns against pity.

> One should hold fast to one's heart; for if one lets it go, how soon one loses one's head, too!
> Alas, where in the world have there been greater follies than with the compassionate? And what in the world has caused more suffering than the follies of the compassionate?
> Woe to all lovers who cannot surmount pity!
> Thus spoke the Devil to me once: 'Even God has his Hell: it is his love for man.'
> And I lately heard him say these words: 'God is dead; God has died of his pity for man.'
> So be warned against pity: *thence* shall yet come a heavy cloud for man! Truly, I understand weather-signs!
> But mark, too, this saying: All great love is above pity: for it wants – to create what is loved!
> 'I offer myself to my love, *and my neighbour as myself*' – that is the language of all creators.
> All creators, however, are hard.

> Thus spoke Zarathustra.

> F. Nietzsche, *Thus Spoke Zarathustra* (1883–91), part 2, 'Of the Compassionate'.

Nietzsche in fact loathed the Kaiser's Germany, but Heinrich von Treitschke was a leading nineteenth-century advocate of German unity under Prussian leadership. He and many of his fellow academics (the 'mad professors' who were often to be jeered at by British propagandists) argued that *Kultur* could and would dominate the world, overtaking British influence because Britain only cared about money. Physical force would be necessary, a view put especially clearly by General von Bernhardi in *Germany and the Next War* (1912), a book which drew so much horrified attention in Britain that the translation was reprinted eleven times before 1914. Bernhardi's most notorious claims were that war (which he expected to be started by Britain) was 'a biological necessity' and that Germany's future was 'world-power or downfall'.

War is a biological necessity of the first importance, a regulative element in the life of mankind which cannot be dispensed with, since without it an unhealthy development will follow, which excludes every advancement of the race, and therefore all real civilization. 'War is the father of all things' [Heraclitus]. The sages of antiquity long before Darwin recognized this.

The struggle for existence is, in the life of Nature, the basis of all healthy development. All existing things show themselves to be the result of contesting forces. So in the life of man the struggle is not merely the destructive, but the life-giving principle. 'To supplant or to be supplanted is the essence of life,' says Goethe, and the strong life gains the upper hand. The law of the stronger holds good everywhere. Those forms survive which are able to procure themselves the most favourable conditions of life, and to assert themselves in the universal economy of Nature. The weaker succumb. This struggle is regulated and restrained by the unconscious sway of biological laws and by the interplay of opposite forces. In the plant world and the animal world this process is worked out in unconscious tragedy. In the human race it is consciously carried out, and regulated by social ordinances. The man of strong will and strong intellect tries by every means to assert himself, the ambitious strive to rise, and in

this effort the individual is far from being guided
merely by the consciousness of right. The life-work
and the life-struggle of many men are determined,
doubtless, by unselfish and ideal motives, but to a far
greater extent the less noble passions – craving for
possessions, enjoyment and honour, envy and the
thirst for revenge – determine men's actions. Still more
often, perhaps, it is the need to live which brings down
even natures of a higher mould into the universal
struggle for existence and enjoyment. . . .

Struggle is, therefore, a universal law of Nature, and
the instinct of self-preservation which leads to struggle
is acknowledged to be a natural condition of existence.
'Man is a fighter.' Self-sacrifice is a renunciation of
life, whether in the existence of the individual or
in the life of States, which are agglomerations of
individuals. The first and paramount law is the
assertion of one's own independent existence. By self-
assertion alone can the State maintain the conditions
of life for its citizens, and insure them the legal
protection which each man is entitled to claim from
it. This duty of self-assertion is by no means satisfied
by the mere repulse of hostile attacks; it includes
the obligation to assure the possibility of life and
development to the whole body of the nation embraced
by the State.

Strong, healthy, and flourishing nations increase in
numbers. From a given moment they require a continual expansion of their frontiers, they require new
territory for the accommodation of their surplus population. Since almost every part of the globe is inhabited,
new territory must, as a rule, be obtained at the cost
of its possessors – that is to say, by conquest, which
thus becomes a law of necessity.

The right of conquest is universally acknowledged.
At first the procedure is pacific. Over-populated
countries pour a stream of emigrants into other States
and territories. These submit to the legislature of the
new country, but try to obtain favourable conditions
of existence for themselves at the cost of the original

inhabitants, with whom they compete. This amounts to conquest.

The right of colonization is also recognized. Vast territories inhabited by uncivilized masses are occupied by more highly civilized States, and made subject to their rule. Higher civilization and the correspondingly greater power are the foundations of the right to annexation . . .

> Friedrich von Bernhardi, *Germany and the Next War* (1912), pp.18–19, 21–23.

Some British commentators maintained that ever since Frederick the Great, Prussian *Kultur* had discarded Christianity in favour of 'blood and iron' (Bismarck's phrase) and the doctrine that 'Might is Right'. Nevertheless, they tended to share the 'Darwinist' view, which had originated in Britain though not from Darwin, that human progress depends on struggle within the species. Other people said that fears about Germany were foolishly 'alarmist'. When war finally arrived, writers of very varied political beliefs – Edward Carpenter, H. A. L. Fisher, and the Bishop of London among them – quoted the following declaration by a nineteenth-century Prussian general as a typical example of long-standing 'Prussianism'.

Do not let us forget the civilizing task which the decrees of Providence have assigned to us. Just as Prussia was destined to be the nucleus of Germany, so the regenerated Germany shall be the nucleus of a future Empire of the West. And in order that no one shall be left in doubt, we proclaim from henceforth that our continental nation has a right to the sea, not only to the North Sea, but to the Mediterranean and Atlantic. Hence we intend to absorb one after another all the provinces which neighbour on Prussia. We will successively annex Denmark, Holland, Belgium, Northern Switzerland, then Trieste and Venice, finally Northern France from the Sambre to the Loire. This programme we fearlessly pronounce. It is not the work of a madman. The Empire we intend to found will be no Utopia. We have ready to our hands the means of founding it, and no coalition in the world can stop us.

Bronsart von Schellendorf, quoted in Edward Carpenter, *The Healing of Nations* (1915), p.79.

D. H. Lawrence was one of many British writers who were repelled by Prussian militarism before the war. His short story, 'The Prussian Officer', was written in Bavaria in 1913, although the title was not added until publication in December 1914 in an attempt to catch the surge in demand for anti-Prussian books. The story is of an officer whose strong but unacknowledged sexual feelings towards his servant are expressed in violence. Such subjects were still scarcely permissible in fiction. Lawrence was reflecting the new interest in sexual psychology, a field which was, in fact, being pioneered by German and Austrian researchers (some of Freud's most important work was in progress during these years); he was also drawing on recent German scandals about cruelty in the army and homosexuality at court.

[The orderly] had a scar on his left thumb, a deep seam going across the knuckle. The officer had long suffered from it, and wanted to do something to it. Still it was there, ugly and brutal on the young, brown hand. At last the Captain's reserve gave way. One day, as the orderly was smoothing out the tablecloth, the officer pinned down this thumb with a pencil, asking:
'How did you come by that?'
The young man winced and drew back at attention.
'A wood axe, Herr Hauptmann,' he answered.
The officer waited for further explanation. None came. The orderly went about his duties. The elder man was sullenly angry. His servant avoided him. And the next day he had to use all his will-power to avoid seeing the scarred thumb. He wanted to get hold of it and—— A hot flame ran in his blood.
He knew his servant would soon be free, and would be glad. As yet, the soldier had held himself off from

the elder man. The Captain grew madly irritable. He could not rest when the soldier was away, and when he was present, he glared at him with tormented eyes. He hated those fine, black brows over the unmeaning, dark eyes, he was infuriated by the free movement of the handsome limbs, which no military discipline could make stiff. And he became harsh and cruelly bullying, using contempt and satire. The young soldier only grew more mute and expressionless.

'What cattle were you bred by, that you can't keep straight eyes? Look me in the eyes when I speak to you.'

And the soldier turned his dark eyes to the other's face, but there was no sight in them: he stared with the slightest possible cast, holding back his sight, perceiving the blue of his master's eyes, but receiving no look from them. And the elder man went pale, and his reddish eyebrows twitched. He gave his order, barrenly.

Once he flung a heavy military glove into the young soldier's face. Then he had the satisfaction of seeing the black eyes flare up into his own, like a blaze when straw is thrown on a fire. And he had laughed with a little tremor and a sneer.

D. H. Lawrence, *The Prussian Officer and Other Stories* (1914).

Allied propagandists were to portray Germany as riddled with cruelty, sexual deviance and a morbid interest in psychology. Ironically, Lawrence himself, with his German wife and strange modern ideas, was to come under suspicion as a German spy.

Ready or Not?

Some writers, both British and German, argued before the war that Britain's nerve and influence were failing. The Germans strongly condemned the campaign against the Boers in South Africa, an issue on which British opinion was itself bitterly divided, and they observed the growing pressure for independence in India. The Liberal election victory in 1906 led to a new concern with home affairs. The Liberals introduced old-age pensions and the beginnings of the Welfare State. They also carried out extensive defence reforms, but these were not enough to satisfy nationalists such as the explorer and poet, Charles Doughty, whose verse drama, *The Cliffs*, opens with German spies landing on the unguarded coast of what they call 'Petticoat Island' and coolly discussing invasion plans. Mythological scenes follow, beginning with a symbolic vision of Britain's current decay.

> *In a sea mist, which is streaming over the Cliff, there gathers form the appearance of a Temple; in whose porch stands the Sacred Image, on a pedestal, of Britannia: and in the Precinct, which is before the Temple-steps, is seen the likeness of an Altar of Incense. The walls of Britannias Temple are rent, and lean forth, as ready to fall; the courses of her building-stones are unknit. The joints of her pillars are broken and out of frame. Her Altar, cold and moss-grown, is blackened now only of the rain of heaven. Upon the altar sides, are seen graven, in partly effaced letters,* RELIGION *and* PATRIOTISM.
> *Britannias helmed Image languishes, under heavy constraining boughts of a monstrous Serpent. Her august front is blindfold with a thick veil.*

Charles Doughty, *The Cliffs* (1909), p.67.

The obscurity of plot and language thickens, but in the end a band of patriots raises a citizen army and the invasion fleet retires. Doughty calls for individual and communal heroism, based on courage, honour and a sense of tradition. These 'manly' virtues had been given famous expression by Henry Newbolt in poems written for the edification of the young.

> This is the Chapel: here, my son,
>   Your father thought the thoughts of youth,
> And heard the words that one by one
>   The touch of Life has turned to truth.

Here in a day that is not far,
  You too may speak with noble ghosts
Of manhood and the vows of war
  You made before the Lord of Hosts.

To set the cause above renown,
  To love the game beyond the prize,
To honour, while you strike him down,
  The foe that comes with fearless eyes;
To count the life of battle good,
  And dear the land that gave you birth,
And dearer yet the brotherhood
  That binds the brave of all the earth –

My son, the oath is yours: the end
  Is His, Who built the world of strife,
Who gave His children Pain for friend,
  And Death for surest hope of life.
To-day and here the fight's begun,
  Of the great fellowship you're free;
Henceforth the School and you are one,
  And what You are, the race shall be.

God send you fortune: yet be sure,
  Among the lights that gleam and pass,
You'll live to follow none more pure
  Than that which glows on yonder brass.
"*Qui procul hinc*," the legend's writ, –
  The frontier-grave is far away –
"*Qui ante diem periit:*
  Sed miles, sed pro patriâ."

Henry Newbolt, 'Clifton Chapel', *The Island
Race* (1898).

The 'pure' message from the public school chapel is that the
dead man 'perished far from here and before his time, but as
a soldier and for the fatherland'. Newbolt's poems sum up
the values that were to enable many people to regard the
Great War as a means of national cleansing and revival.

Needing heroes, the country found one in Captain Scott, who reached the South Pole in 1912 but failed to get there first or to return alive. This double failure made him not just a hero but a tragic one, enthralling the imaginations of those who believed that man had been given 'Pain for friend'. Facsimiles of Scott's last message were hung in classrooms.

> We are weak, writing is difficult, but for my own sake I do not regret this journey which has shewn that Englishmen can endure hardships, help one another, and meet death with as great a fortitude as ever in the past. We took risks, we knew we took them; things have come out against us, and therefore we have no cause for complaint, but bow to the will of Providence, determined still to do our best to the last. . . . Had we lived, I should have had a tale to tell of the hardihood, endurance, and courage of my companions which would have stirred the heart of every Englishman. These rough notes and our dead bodies must tell the tale, but surely, surely, a great rich country like ours will see that those who are dependent on us are properly provided for.

> Robert Scott, last message, 1912.

One of the memorial books published at the time ominously concluded that the 'nation's loss is also the nation's splendid gain. The bones of heroes are also the glorious seeds of heroes to come'.

Scott's expedition appealed to those Britons who thought that the Victorian values of action and duty had given way to talk, grumbling, laziness and rule by complacent 'old men'. There was a campaign for 'National Efficiency'. Charles Sorley, still a schoolboy but soon to become a well-known war poet, was one of many young men who apparently shared this kind of thinking.

> It needs no thought to understand,
>   No speech to tell, no sight to see
> That there has come upon our land
>   The curse of inactivity.

We do not see the vital point
That 'tis the eighth, most deadly, sin
To wail, 'The world is out of joint' –
And not attempt to put it in . . .

We question, answer, make defence,
We sneer, we scoff, we criticise,
We wail and moan our decadence,
Enquire, investigate, surmise;

We preach and prattle, peer and pry
And fit together two and two;
We ponder, argue, shout, swear, lie –
We will not, for we cannot, DO.

Pale puny soldiers of the pen,
Absorbed in this your inky strife,
Act as of old, when men were men,
England herself and life yet life.

> Charles Hamilton Sorley, 'A Call to Action',
> *The Marlburian* (31 October 1912).

Sorley did not abandon this attitude when war broke out, although he eventually decided that Germany was efficient where Britain was tolerant, and that of the two virtues tolerance was superior.

One element in the general concern for efficiency in the decade or so before the war was a loud but unsuccessful campaign for conscription, on the grounds that Britain's small volunteer army would be useless and its huge navy largely irrelevant in a war against the vast conscripted armies of the Continental powers. From 1905 the campaign was led by the famous old soldier, Earl Roberts of Kandahar, who was fiercely criticised by the Left but warmly supported by Kipling and others. Roberts argued in a 1912 speech that the Manchester Free Traders, Cobden and Bright, had been mistaken in supposing that Free Trade would result in disarmament, pointing out (with doubtful logic) that even while they had been putting their case Prussia had been preparing to attack France.

> Such . . . was history's ironic comment upon John Bright's and Richard Cobden's eloquently urged policy. No words of mine can increase the crushing weight of Destiny's criticism.
>
> Now, gentlemen, at the present day, now in the year 1912, just as in 1866 and just as in 1870, war will take place the instant the German forces by land and sea are, by their superiority at every point, as certain of victory as anything in human calculations can be made certain. "Germany strikes when Germany's hour has struck." That is the time honoured policy of her Foreign Office. That was the policy relentlessly pursued by Bismarck and Moltke in 1866 and 1870; it has been her policy decade by decade since that date; it is her policy at the present hour. . . . We may stand still. Germany always advances and the direction of her advance, the line along which she is moving, is now most manifest. It is towards that consummation which I have described – a complete supremacy by land and sea. She has built a mighty fleet; but, as if nothing were done so long as anything stands between her and her goal, still she presses on – here establishing a new Heligoland – for every available island in the North Sea has now been strongly fortified – there encircling Holland in a network of new canals, and deepening old river beds for the swifter transport of the munitions of war, whether to her Army or her Navy. Contrasted with our own apathy or puerile and spasmodic efforts, how impressive is this magnificent and unresting energy! It has the mark of true greatness; it extorts the admiration even from those against whom it is directed! . . .
>
> Gentlemen, only the other day I completed my eightieth year . . . and the words I am speaking to-day are, therefore, old words – the result of years of earnest thought and practical experience. But, Gentlemen, my fellow-citizens and fellow-Britishers, citizens

of this great and sacred trust, this Empire, if these were my last words, I still should say to you – "arm yourselves" and if I put to myself the question, How can I, even at this late and solemn hour, best help England, – England that to me has been so much, England that for me has done so much – again I say, "Arm and prepare to acquit yourselves like men, for the day of your ordeal is at hand." . . .

> Lord Roberts, speech for the National Service
> League, Manchester, October 1912.

'The Great Illusion'?

Roberts's reference to Cobden and Bright was perhaps intended as a criticism of their successor, Norman Angell, who brilliantly restated their views in *The Great Illusion* (1909). The illusion which Angell sought to dispel was that Germany, or any other country, could gain economic advantage from modern war. Many people, including Roberts, had said that a just war might ennoble the British spirit, but it was assumed that Germany's motive for starting hostilities would be purely materialistic.

Angell gave little weight to any idealisms, disarming his opponents by agreeing that idealistic pacifism was unconvincing; his appeal was to financial self-interest. In a world of growing international trade, he said, any nation which damaged a trading partner would be damaging itself; nothing could be gained by capturing territory.

[As] the only possible policy in our day for a conqueror to pursue is to leave the wealth of a territory in the complete possession of the individuals inhabiting that territory, it is a logical fallacy and an optical illusion in Europe to regard a nation as increasing its wealth when it increases its territory, because when a province or State is annexed, the population, who are the real and only owners of the wealth therein, are also annexed, and the conqueror gets nothing. The facts of modern history abundantly demonstrate this.

Norman Angell, *The Great Illusion* (1911 edn), p.31.

The states most attractive to investors were the small ones which were not heavily armed, not the big ones which were devoting so much of their wealth to military preparations. The 'Darwinist' argument for war was absurd.

> [The] more a nation's wealth is protected the less secure does it become.
>
> It is this last fact, constituting as it does one of the most remarkable of economic-sociological phenomena in Europe, which might be made the text of this book. Here we are told by all the experts that great navies and great armies are necessary to protect our wealth against the aggression of powerful neighbours, whose cupidity and voracity can be controlled by force alone; that treaties avail nothing, and that in international politics might makes right. Yet when the financial genius of Europe, studying the question in its purely financial and material aspect, has to decide between the great States, with all their imposing paraphernalia of colossal armies and fabulously costly navies, and the little States (which, if our political pundits are right, could any day have their wealth gobbled up by those voracious big neighbours), possessing relatively no military power whatever, such genius plumps solidly, and with what is in the circumstances a tremendous difference, in favour of the small and helpless.

Ibid., pp.32–3.

Angell was convinced that business interests wanted peace; he would not have agreed with the later claim, still sometimes heard, that the Great War was the creation of financiers. Nor was he impressed by the warlike talk of Germans such as Bernhardi; he showed in 1914 that equally fearsome declarations had come from British sources.

We deem the crime of Germany fully proved because Bernhardi writes of "world-power or downfall," but when one of our own Oxford professors writes that England has no alternative between the leadership of the human race and loss of her empire, we accept it as a quite natural and laudable political conception; and we are horrified at German adulation of war as a noble thing in itself; but our own poets and clergymen urge just that thing, and we are not horrified at all. We point to German hostility to peace as a proof of her ineradicable barbarism, while our own popular journalists have for years poured ferocious contempt upon "the amiable sentimentalists at The Hague with their impossible dreams of arbitration and disarmament."

> Norman Angell, 'The Prussian Within Our Midst', *Prussianism and its Destruction* (1914), p.98.

Unease in the Arts

Many poets and novelists were as sceptical as Angell about the value of war and violent action, although they sometimes felt guilty about their own detachment. One of the shrewdest observers of the age, E. M. Forster, symbolised the awkward union between thinkers and doers in his novel *Howards End* (1910), in which Margaret Schlegel, who believes in culture, intellect and personal relationships, marries Henry Wilcox, the representative of efficiency, business and empire. Margaret is half-German but not in the least 'Prussian'. Looking down on Poole harbour, the Schlegel sisters meditate on England.

> The water crept over the mud-flats towards the gorse and the blackened heather. Branksea Island lost its immense foreshores, and became a sombre episode of trees. Frome was forced inwards towards Dorchester, Stour against Wimborne, Avon towards Salisbury, and

over the immense displacement the sun presided, leading it to triumph ere he sank to rest. England was alive, throbbing through all her estuaries, crying for joy through the mouths of all her gulls, and the north wind, with contrary motion, blew stronger against her rising seas. What did it mean? For what end are her fair complexities, her changes of soil, her sinuous coast? Does she belong to those who have moulded her and made her feared by other lands, or to those who have added nothing to her power, but have somehow seen her, seen the whole island at once, lying as a jewel in a silver sea, sailing as a ship of souls, with all the brave world's fleet accompanying her towards eternity?

E. M. Forster, *Howards End* (1910), chapter 19.

The places are in Hardy's Wessex and some of the language is from Shakespeare ('This precious stone set in the silver sea'); Forster and the Schlegels 'see' the England of the poets, feeling love, bafflement and apprehension as the ship of souls moves on into change, darkness and a rising wind.

The sentiment of that passage from *Howards End* is characteristic of the new 'Georgian' poets, such as John Masefield, Rupert Brooke and, after 1914, Edward Thomas. Perhaps the most famous of the many contemporary expressions of the Georgian way of 'seeing' England is Brooke's 'The Old Vicarage, Grantchester'.

> Ah God! to see the branches stir
> Across the moon at Grantchester!
> To smell the thrilling-sweet and rotten
> Unforgettable, unforgotten
> River-smell, and hear the breeze
> Sobbing in the little trees.
> Say, do the elm-clumps greatly stand
> Still guardians of that holy land?
> The chestnuts shade, in reverend dream,
> The yet unacademic stream?
> Is dawn a secret shy and cold

Anadyomene, silver-gold?
And sunset still a golden sea
From Haslingfield to Madingley?
And after, ere the night is born,
Do hares come out about the corn?
Oh, is the water sweet and cool,
Gentle and brown, above the pool?
And laughs the immortal river still
Under the mill, under the mill?
Say, is there Beauty yet to find?
And Certainty? and Quiet kind?
Deep meadows yet, for to forget
The lies, and truths, and pain? . . . Oh! yet
Stands the Church clock at ten to three?
And is there honey still for tea?

> Rupert Brooke, 'The Old Vicarage,
> Grantchester' (1912), ll.115–40.

'Grantchester' is a less peaceful poem than it seems. It is consciously 'modern' writing, its blunt informality challenging the traditional diction of much Edwardian verse; composed in Berlin in May 1912 it is indeed Georgian, just into the new reign. It is also anti-German, as its opening section makes clear, and the unregulated Cambridge countryside is evoked as a contrast to the mechanical discipline of urban Germany. In a period that was often to be looked back on as the last golden summer before Europe plunged into a long winter, Brooke expresses a general fear that time will not stand still.

Contemporary readers could recognise Brooke's style as mildly revolutionary. Poetry was changing fast, responding like the other arts to the world's unease. 'Grantchester' was included in Edward Marsh's *Georgian Poetry 1911–1912* (December 1912), an anthology of new verse that became an instant success. Declaring his 'belief that English poetry is now once again putting on a new strength and beauty', Marsh selected work by young authors who were in rebellion against both the matter and the manner of Victorian and Edwardian writing. The Georgians held that poetry should deal with true experience, including violence if necessary, in 'the real language of men'. Several of them, notably Masefield and W. W. Gibson, described scenes from working-class life, trying to capture the words and rhythms of colloquial speech. Their work laid the foundations for many of the war poems that were to be written by later Georgians such as Sassoon, Graves and Robert Nichols. Much of the 1914–18 poetry that is still read today is either by Georgians or by poets who were strongly influenced by Georgians.

British taste was too moderate and too insular to permit the wide acceptance of more radical movements. Comparatively few war poems were to be written by the Imagists, another literary group who established themselves in the years immediately before 1914. Imagist poetry was too 'modern' to appeal to the vast but temporary demand for verse which the war created, although it prepared the way for the success of T. S. Eliot and other 'Modernists' in the twenties. Unlike the Georgians, the Imagists were strongly interested in developments abroad, where political turmoil was matched by upheavals in all the arts. The Cubists and Post-Impressionists had revolutionised painting. Music was changing profoundly with the work of Stravinsky and Schoenberg. The fiercest assault on accepted values had come from the Italian Futurists, whose first Manifesto (1909) declared their faith in speed, machinery and war. They said that poetry should 'exalt aggressive action, a feverish insomnia, the racer's stride, the mortal leap, the punch and the slap' and should 'glorify war – the world's only hygiene – militarism, patriotism, the destructive gesture of freedom-bringers, beautiful ideas worth dying for'. Futurism expressed especially clearly the hunger for violent change which had been growing for decades in reaction to the stuffy respectability of bourgeois Europe. The quieter changes in the arts in Britain were part of the general social and cultural turbulence of the West.

Last-minute Warnings

By 1913 war seemed frighteningly probable. Worried authors published grim, sometimes gruesome accounts of what a war might be like; their work was hastily written and soon swept away, but it shows that the horrors were dreaded and at least approximately foreseen by some people before August 1914. Alfred Noyes, for example, described the mass slaughter of young men by the machine guns of an invisible enemy.

> Then all along the reeking hills
>   And up the dark ravines,
> The long rows of young men
> Leapt in the glory of life again
> To carry their warm and breathing breasts
>   Against the cold machines;
>
> Against the Death that mowed them down
>   With a cold indifferent hand;
> And every gap at once was fed
> With more life from the fountain-head,
> Filled up from endless ranks behind
>   In the name of the Fatherland,
>
> Mown down! Mown down! Mown down! Mown
>   down!
>   They staggered in sheets of fire,
> They reeled like ships in a sudden blast,
> And shreds of flesh went spattering past,
> And the hoarse bugles laughed on high,
>   Like fiends from hell – *Retire!*
>
> The tall young men, the tall young men,
>   That were so fain to die,
> It was not theirs to question,
>   It was not theirs to reply.
>
> They had broken their hearts on the cold machines;
>   And – they had not seen their foe;
> And the reason of this butcher's work

It was not theirs to know;
For these tall young men were children
Five short years ago.

> Alfred Noyes, *The Wine-Press: A Tale of War*
> (1913), pp.42–3.

The Wine-Press is now forgotten, as is W. D. Newton's *War* (early 1914), a clumsy novel about invasion which seeks to show how war would destroy the social and moral order which British people had taken for granted for so long. Newton carefully avoids any reference to nationalities; like Noyes, he is not propagandising against Germany, but he uses as his preface part of a 1913 speech by Kipling. After describing the chaos that invasion would bring, Kipling had called for strong deterrence, a theme he had spoken on many times before.

It is almost as impossible to make a people who have never known invasion realize what invasion is as it is to make a man realize the fact of his own death. The nearest a man can come in imagination to his own death is the idea of lying in a coffin with his eyes shut listening to the pleasant things he thinks his neighbours are saying about him; and the nearest that a people who have never known conquest or invasion can come to the idea of conquest and invasion is a hazy notion of going about their usual work and paying their taxes to tax collectors who will perhaps talk with a slightly foreign accent. Even attempted invasion does not mean that; it means riot and arson and disorder and bloodshed and starvation on a scale that a man can scarcely imagine to himself; it means disorganization of every relation of life and every walk of business from the highest to the lowest, and the more elaborate the civilization the more awful will be the disorganization – in other words, what the Balkan States can stand for twelve months and still breathe would knock us out of time in six weeks.
It seems to me that if there is a reasonable chance –

and I think there is – of such a catastrophe overtaking us, we ought at least to take reasonable precautions to make any attempted invasion so exceedingly expensive to begin with and so particularly unpleasant to go on with, that no enemy would think of facing the risk. As things stand at present we have neither the men nor the means nor the organization nor the will to produce such results. That is why those of us who think go about in fear and in doubt; that is why those of us who do not think are full of silly boastings one day and of blind panic the next; that is why we have no security inside or outside our borders; that is why we tell each other lies to cover our own fears and yet know all the time that our lies are useless.

In this matter we must take refuge behind no self-paid member of Parliament. The power to change this wasteful state of affairs lies in the hands of the people of England. The responsibility is ours and the punishment if we persist in our folly, in our fraud, and in our make-believe – the punishment with fall not only upon us but upon the third and fourth generation of those that have betrayed their country.

Rudyard Kipling, speech for the National Service League (1913).

The Prime Minister, H. H. Asquith, and his Liberal colleagues had worked for peace, trying to calm fears about Germany and to avoid getting caught up in the arms race. Despite their efforts, they were attacked from the Right as liars and 'betrayers of their country' (it is hardly surprising that they detested Kipling) and from the Left as servants of capitalism and imperialism. Several crises which could have led to war had been overcome, but when the heir to the Austro-Hungarian Empire was assassinated in Sarajevo on 28 June 1914 perhaps no British Government could have prevented what followed. Austria blamed Serbia. 'TO HELL WITH SERBIA', thundered the popular newspaper, *John Bull*, representing the British lack of interest in East European affairs, but Austria's declaration of war against Serbia on 26

July made all Europe realise that many nations could be drawn in. 'THE WAR MUST BE STOPPED', said *The Labour Leader*, the voice of the radical Independent Labour Party, 'AND WE MUST STOP IT'.

[The] danger of a great European War is very real. Should this terrible possibility become an actual fact, it is beyond human imagination to conceive the horror of the events that would ensue. Death, disease, starvation would reign over the entire Continent, and, unless the war were stopped in its early stages, the whole fabric of civilisation in Europe would fall to the ground. The armies which would engage in conflict would number seven million men. On the North Sea, in the English Channel, on the Baltic Sea, in the Mediterranean, the naval fleets of the two groups would meet with unthinkable disaster. Cities would be destroyed, the countryside would be devastated, food supplies would be cut off, the people would starve in thousands and rise in hungry rebellion. Every man's hand would be against his brother's.

A very grave responsibility rests upon the Socialist and Labour movement of Europe at this moment. Our movement is the guardian of peace. It is fifty million strong, and if it will only act unitedly it can make war impossible.

If the organised workers will demonstrate with sufficient force, a European war can be made absolutely impossible. No nation which is divided against itself can expect to wage war successfully with another nation. On the Continent, where the armies are Conscriptionist, this is particularly true, and it is an open secret that thousands of the soldiers serving the German, French, and Austrian Governments by compulsion are Socialists and view their task with loathing and abhorrence. Victories cannot be won with armies of that nature.

Unless we are thought to be exaggerating the influence of the Labour and Socialist movement, we will quote from the Liberal weekly review, *The Nation*. In its issue of May 17, of this year, it said:

> 'We believe that the influence of Socialism is now so widespread as to be a check upon any war for any end save a defence so legitimate and inevitable that even a Socialist conscience would regretfully approve it.'

No Socialist conscience would approve the war which is looming before us if it came upon us. We have the power to stop it. We must do so.

The Labour Leader, front-page editorial, 30 July 1914.

War Declared

It was too late. Serbia appealed to Russia. Russia mobilised. Fearing encirclement and believing that Britain might remain neutral, the Kaiser decided to join Austria and to make pre-emptive attacks on Russia and France. A highly efficient German army suddenly crashed through neutral Luxembourg into neutral Belgium on its way to the French frontier. France called for British aid, ordering her forces to stay well within French territory as proof that she was the victim of aggression. Up to the last minute the British Government tried to mediate but did not declare its intentions. The Cabinet had been divided, with Lloyd George, Churchill and others arguing that the country should keep out of a European conflict. In the end, all but two ministers agreed that the assault on Belgium, whose neutrality had been confirmed by Britain and Germany in an 1893 treaty, had closed all peaceful options. On 3 August the Foreign Secretary, Sir Edward Grey, announced to a tense House of Commons that Germany had to choose between immediate withdrawal from Belgium and a British declaration of war. His speech was low-key and now sounds a little flustered, but it was warmly received as a properly British statement at last. It was the supreme moment of Grey's career, for the tardiness of his decision and certain admissions in his speech left him vulnerable to increasing hostility later on. He said that he had told the French authorities long before that in the event of German aggression against France Britain might be expected to come to her support if public opinion allowed. 'Secret diplomacy' of this kind was to lay him open to the charge of having committed the country to war without even having consulted his colleagues. However, in the excitement of 3 August Grey's critics in the Commons were disregarded. He ended his speech by calling for courage and endurance.

> The most awful responsibility is resting upon the Government in deciding what to advise the House of Commons to do. We have disclosed our mind to the House of Commons. We have disclosed the issue, the information which we have, and made clear to the House, I trust, that we are prepared to face that situation, and that should it develop, as probably it may develop, we will face it. We worked for peace up to the last moment, and beyond the last moment. How hard, how persistently, and how earnestly we strove for peace last week, the House will see from the papers that will be before it.
>
> But that is over, as far as the peace of Europe is concerned. We are now face to face with a situation and all the consequences which it may yet have to unfold. We believe we shall have the support of the House at large in proceeding to whatever the consequences may be and whatever measures may be forced upon us by the development of facts or action taken by others. I believe the country, so quickly has the situation been forced upon it, has not had time to realise the issue. It perhaps is still thinking of the quarrel between Austria and Servia, and not the complications of this matter which have grown out of the quarrel between Austria and Servia. Russia and Germany we know are at war. We do not yet know officially that Austria, the ally whom Germany is to support, is yet at war with Russia. We know that a good deal has been happening on the French frontier.

We do not know that the German Ambassador has left Paris.

The situation has developed so rapidly that technically, as regards the condition of the war, it is most difficult to describe what has actually happened. I wanted to bring out the underlying issues which would affect our own conduct, and our own policy, and to put them clearly. I have put the vital facts before the House, and if, as seems not improbable, we are forced, and rapidly forced, to take our stand upon those issues, then I believe, when the country realises what is at stake, what the real issues are, the magnitude of the impending dangers in the West of Europe, which I have endeavoured to describe to the House, we shall be supported throughout, not only by the House of Commons, but by the determination, the resolution, the courage, and the endurance of the whole country.

> Edward Grey, speech to the House of Commons, 3 August 1914, quoted in *Through Terror to Triumph* (1914), pp.24–6.

Among the journalists who heard the Foreign Secretary's speech was H. H. Munro, better remembered by the pen-name 'Saki' which he used for his satirical short stories. Munro's politics were sternly patriotic; he had supported Lord Roberts's campaign for conscription and had written a novel, *When William Came* (1913), which described Britain feebly acquiescing after a successful German invasion. The report which he sent to his newspaper expresses a relief which was widely felt.

For one memorable and uncomfortable hour the House of Commons had the attention of the nation and most of the world concentrated on it. Grey's speech, when one looked back at it, was a statesman-like utterance, delivered in an excellent manner, dignified and convincing. To sit listening to it, in uncertainty for a long time as to what line of policy it was going to announce, with all the accumulated doubts and suspicions of the previous forty-eight hours heavy on one's mind, was an experience that one would not care to repeat often in a lifetime. Men who read it as it was spelled out jerkily on the tape-machines, letter by letter, told me that the strain of uncertainty was even more cruel; and I can well believe it. When the actual tenor of the speech became clear, and one knew beyond a doubt where we stood, there was only room for one feeling; the miserable tension of the past two days had been removed, and one discovered that one was slowly recapturing the lost sensation of being in a good temper.

> H. H. Munro ('Saki'), report dated 3 August,
> *Outlook*, 8 August 1914, quoted in A. J.
> Langguth, *Saki* (1981), pp.247–8.

Munro made immediate preparations to enlist in the ranks, even though he was over age (he was killed on the Somme in 1916). Few people believed that Germany would evacuate Belgium. Once the war machine had started, there was no peaceful means of stopping it. On 4 August Britain formally declared war.

> Owing to the summary rejection by the German Government of the request made by his Majesty's Government for assurances that the neutrality of Belgium will be respected, his Majesty's Ambassador in Berlin has received his passports and his Majesty's Government have declared to the German Government that a state of war exists between Great Britain and Germany as from 11 p.m. on August 4.

> Statement from the Foreign Office, London, 4
> August 1914.

Grey's stipulation that Britain could only enter a European war if such a move had popular support was amply met. Public opinion had been ahead of the Government; Serbia might go to hell, but not little Belgium. Lloyd George later described the general enthusiasm.

The theory which is propagated to-day by pacifist orators of the more cantankerous and less convincing type that the Great War was engineered by elder and middle-aged statesmen who sent younger men to face its horrors, is an invention. The elder statesmen did their feckless best to prevent war, whilst the youth of the rival countries were howling impatiently at their doors for immediate war. I saw it myself during the first four days of August, 1914. I shall never forget the warlike crowds that thronged Whitehall and poured into Downing Street, whilst the Cabinet was deliberating on the alternative of peace or war. On Sunday there was a great crowd. Monday was Bank Holiday, and multitudes of young people concentrated in Westminster demonstrating for war against Germany. We could hear the hum of this surging mass from the Cabinet Chamber. On Monday afternoon I walked with Mr. Asquith to the House of Commons to hear Grey's famous speech. The crowd was so dense that no car could drive through it, and had it not been for police assistance we could not have walked a yard on our way. It was distinctly a pro-war demonstration. I remember observing at the time: "These people are very anxious to send our poor soldiers to face death; how many of them will ever go into battle themselves?" It was an unworthy doubt of the courage and patriotism of the demonstrators. A few days later recruiting stands were set up in the Horse Guards Parade, and that great open space beheld a crowd of young men surging around these stands and pushing their way through to give their names for enlistment in the Kitchener Armies. For days I heard, from the windows of Downing Street and the Treasury, the movement of a myriad feet towards the stands and the shouting of names of eager volunteers by the recruiting sergeants. The War had leapt into popularity between Saturday and Monday. On Saturday the Governor of the Bank of England called on me, as Chancellor of the Exchequer, to inform me on behalf of the City that the financial and trading interests in the City of London

were totally opposed to our intervening in the War. By
Monday there was a complete change. The threatened
invasion of Belgium had set the nation on fire from
sea to sea.

David Lloyd George, *War Memoirs* (1938), vol.1,
pp.39–40.

The liberation of Belgium was to remain Britain's supreme
war aim; other countries had more obviously selfish motives.
Until the crusading Americans arrived in 1917, the British
would be able to see themselves as the most moral of the
major belligerents. *The Times* expressed a general mood, but
revealed the element of self-interest that existed in the nation's
purpose from the beginning.

This day will be momentous in the history of all
time. . . . We have refused to do today what Mr
Gladstone [referring to Belgium] told us in 1870
honour and conscience forbade us to do. We have
refused 'quietly to stand by and witness the perpetra-
tion of the direst crime that ever stained the pages of
history, and thus become participants in the sin.' We
are fighting now to save a flourishing constitutional
kingdom which has constantly deserved and enjoyed
our friendship against a wrong no independent State
could tolerate without the loss of all its most essential
liberties. We are going into the war that is forced upon
us as the defenders of the weak and the champions of
the liberties of Europe. We are drawing the sword in
the same cause for which we drew it against Philip II,
against Louis XIV, and against Napoleon. It is the
cause of right and honour, but it is also the cause of
our own vital and immediate interests. The Nether-
lands and Belgium largely owe their independent
existence to the instinct we have ever felt and ever
acted on – that on no account whatever can England
suffer the coasts of the North Sea and of the narrow
seas over against her own to be at the command of a
great military monarchy, be that monarchy which it
may. . . .

We must suffer much, but we shall know how to suffer for the great name of England and for all her high ideals, as our fathers did before us. We go into the fray without hatred, without passion, without selfish ambitions, or selfish ends. We go into it in the spirit which our fellow-subjects in the Dominions have shown with one accord – the spirit in which their King and ours has assured them that he has found fresh strength in this hour of national trial. We go into it 'united, calm, resolute, trusting in God'. That is the mood in which our fathers fought and won. That is the mood in which we, their true sons, will fight today, with the humble but firm hope that in a just and righteous cause 'the only Giver of all victory' will bless our arms.

The Times, leading article, 5 August 1914.

Most people were relieved that the nation's doubts and divisions seemed to be over, hoping that it could now unite in an honourable cause. Alfred Noyes was typical in abandoning his earlier fears and identifying himself with the national effort.

We fought for peace, and we have seen the law
   Cancelled, not once, nor twice, by felon hands,
     But shattered, again, again, and yet again.
We fought for peace. Now, in God's name, we draw
   The sword, not with a riot of flags and bands,
     But silence, and a mustering of men.

They challenge Truth. An Empire makes reply.
   One faith, one flag, one honour, and one might.
   From sea to sea, from height to war worn height,
The old word rings out – to conquer or to die.
And we shall conquer. Though their eagles fly
   Through heaven, around this ancient isle unite
   Powers that were never vanquished in the fight –
The unconquerable powers that cannot lie.

But they who challenge Truth, Law, Justice, all
    The bases on which God and man stand sure
        Throughout all ages; fools! – they thought us torn
So far with discord that the blow might fall
    Unanswered; and, while all those powers endure,
    This is our answer: Unity and Scorn.

Alfred Noyes, 'The United Front', *The Daily
Mail* (6 August 1914).

3 War to End War: August 1914–December 1915

Despite later mythology, most people were neither light-hearted nor blind to danger in the first months of the war. The prevailing spirit in Britain and throughout the Empire was one of co-operation, goodwill and hard work; it was also one of protest, for the invasion of Belgium aroused a deep and honest fury. The colonies raised generous volunteer forces, and at home Lord Kitchener's demand for 'the first hundred thousand' was answered before the month ended, a swift start to the task of mustering armies that were eventually to be numbered in millions. Getting each man uniformed, fed, trained, armed, and positioned in the line was the largest undertaking the country had ever attempted. Authors touring the support lines later were astonished by the vast quantities of neatly marshalled equipment; even among memoirs of front-line troops there are few stories of men on the Western Front being seriously short of food or supplies (the Eastern campaigns were very different). A letter posted in England would normally reach the trenches next day. Little of this could have been achieved without an almost universal readiness to 'do one's bit'.

It has become a commonplace to say that this was 'a literary war'; it might more accurately be described as a war which involved the whole population, literary people along with the rest. Young writers enlisted, while older ones helped in other ways. Henry James, appalled by the conflict, opened his house to Belgian refugees and later took British citizenship as a gesture of support. John Galsworthy, equally distressed, threw himself into patriotic journalism. Arnold Bennett assisted in local anti-invasion plans. Almost everyone looked for something that could be done and set about doing it with fervent energy.

Although the vast majority of British people embarked on

Down with the War!

WORKERS of Great Britain, you have no quarrel with the workers of Europe. They have no quarrel with you. The quarrel is between the RULING Classes of Europe.

DON'T MAKE THEIR QUARREL YOURS.

One Million Trade Unionists and Socialists of Austria have protested against the war.

DON'T DESERT THEM.

Three Million Trade Unionists and Socialists of Germany have protested against the war.

DON'T DESERT THEM.

Workers of Great Britain, unite with the organised workers of France and Russia in saying that though our Governments declare war we declare peace.

Stand true in this hour of crisis. The flag of International Solidarity is greater than the flag of Britain, of Germany, of France, of Austria, or Russia. It waves over all.

Why should you go to war? What have you to gain from war? What has war ever done for you? What did the last war—the Boer War—do for you? Twenty thousand workers were shot dead on the battlefield. You are still paying £12,000,000 every year in food taxes for it. The workers of South Africa are worse off than ever. The rich mineowners alone benefited.

THE WORKERS NEVER BENEFIT BY WAR.

This is not your war. It is not the war of the German working class, or of the French working class, or of the Austrian working class, or of the Russian working class.

It is the war of the British RULING Class, of the German RULING Class, of the French RULING Class, and of the Austrian RULING Class.

IT IS THEIR WAR, NOT YOURS.

This is a war of the RULING Classes. But the RULING Classes will not fight. They will call on you to fight.

Your fathers, your brothers, your sons will be called upon to shoot down the German workers. The German workers will be called upon to shoot down your fathers, your brothers, your sons. You have no quarrel. But you will have to suffer.

WHY SHOULD YOU?

You will have to pay for the war. You will hunger and starve. Your wives will hunger and starve. Your children will hunger and starve.

WHY SHOULD THEY?

Workers, even now you can stop this terrible calamity if you will! No Government can continue to engage in war if its people say with sufficient strength: THERE MUST BE PEACE.

SAY IT!

Say it in your thousands. March through the streets and say it. Gather together in your squares and market places and say it. Say it everywhere. Say it, and go on saying it until the Government heeds.

Workers, don't fail your comrades at this great moment. Stand by your fellow-workers here. Stand by your fellow-workers in Europe. Whoever else deserts the ranks, whatever you may have to face, stand firm. The future is dark, but in the solidarity of the workers lies the hope which shall, once again, bring light to the peoples of Europe.

Down with the War!

The Labour Leader, 6 August 1914.

the war in a spirit of protest against Germany, there was a minority from the start which protested against the war itself as can be seen from the front page of *The Labour Leader* on 6 August (p.38). Such calls found few echoes. Most of the Labour movement in all countries supported the war. Socialist idealism had to face the fact that the workers of the world were not going to unite for peace. Marxism had failed its first great test, but its most committed adherents held their ground. Perhaps the most effective wartime verse-writer of the Left was the journalist, W. N. Ewer, whose 'Five Souls' (3 October 1914) has often been anthologised.

FIRST SOUL
I was a peasant of the Polish plain;
I left my plough because the message ran: –
Russia in danger, needed every man
To save her from the Teuton; and was slain.
I gave my life for freedom – This I know
For those who bade me fight had told me so.

SECOND SOUL
I was a Tyrolese, a mountaineer;
I gladly left my mountain home to fight
Against the brutal treacherous Muscovite;
And died in Poland on a Cossack spear.
I gave my life for freedom – This I know
For those who bade me fight had told me so.

THIRD SOUL
I worked in Lyons at my weaver's loom,
When suddenly the Prussian despot hurled
His felon blow at France and at the world;
Then I went forth to Belgium and my doom.
I gave my life for freedom – This I know
For those who bade me fight had told me so.

FOURTH SOUL
I owned a vineyard by the wooded Main,
Until the Fatherland begirt by foes
Lusting her downfall, called me, and I rose
Swift to the call – and died in far Lorraine.

I gave my life for freedom – This I know
For those who bade me fight had told me so.

FIFTH SOUL

I worked in a great shipyard by the Clyde;
There came a sudden word of wars declared,
Of Belgium, peaceful, helpless, unprepared,
Asking our aid: I joined the ranks, and died.
I gave my life for freedom – This I know
For those who bade me fight had told me so.

W. N. Ewer, 'Five Souls', *The Nation* (3 October 1914).

Political opposition to the war was hampered by new laws, but various pressure groups were started, including the Union of Democratic Control, secretly founded in August but forced to go public when the Press attacked it as a pro-German conspiracy. The UDC's main demand was for parliamentary control over foreign policy; among its members were E. D. Morel, Norman Angell and Ramsay MacDonald. Another group was the No-Conscription Fellowship, founded in November by Fenner Brockway (Editor of *The Labour Leader*) and later chaired by Bertrand Russell. Almost all established literary figures supported the war, but Bernard Shaw soon became notorious as a critic of the Government and the national mood. Although maintaining that now the war had been started it had to be fought and won, his long article, 'Common Sense About the War' (November), condemned secret diplomacy and British 'Junkerism' (the Junkers were the Prussian landowning class, regarded as the embodiment of stupid militarism).

And first, I do not see this war as one which has welded Governments and peoples into complete and sympathetic solidarity as against the common enemy. I see the people of England united in a fierce detestation and defiance of the views and acts of Prussian Junkerism. And I see the German people stirred to the depths by a similar antipathy to English Junkerism, and

angered by the apparent treachery and duplicity of the
attack made on them by us in their extremest peril
from France and Russia. I see both nations duped, but
alas! not quite unwillingly duped, by their Junkers
and Militarists into wreaking on one another the wrath
they should have spent in destroying Junkerism and
Militarism in their own country. And I see the Junkers
and Militarists of England and Germany jumping at
the chance they have longed for in vain for many years
of smashing one another and establishing their own
oligarchy as the dominant military power in the
world. No doubt the heroic remedy for this tragic
misunderstanding is that both armies should shoot
their officers and go home to gather in their harvests
in the villages and make a revolution in the towns; and
though this is not at present a practicable solution, it
must be frankly mentioned, because it or something
like it is always a possibility in a defeated conscript
army if its commanders push it beyond human endurance when its eyes are opening to the fact that in
murdering its neighbors it is biting off its nose to
vex its face, besides riveting the intolerable yoke of
Militarism and Junkerism more tightly than ever on
its own neck. But there is no chance – or, as our
Junkers would put it, no danger – of our soldiers
yielding to such an ecstasy of commonsense. They
have enlisted voluntarily; they are not defeated nor
likely to be; their communications are intact and their
meals reasonably punctual; they are as pugnacious as
their officers; and in fighting Prussia they are fighting
a more deliberate, conscious, tyrannical, personally
insolent, and dangerous Militarism than their own.
Still, even for a voluntary professional army, that
possibility exists, just as for the civilian there is a limit
beyond which taxation, bankruptcy, privation, terror,
and inconvenience cannot be pushed without revolution or a social dissolution more ruinous than submission to conquest. I mention all this, not to make myself
wantonly disagreeable, but because military persons,
thinking naturally that there is nothing like leather,

are now talking of this war as likely to become a permanent institution like the Chamber of Horrors at Madame Tussaud's, forgetting, I think, that the rate of consumption maintained by modern military operations is much greater relatively to the highest possible rate of production maintainable under the restrictions of war time than it has ever been before.

George Bernard Shaw, *What I Really Wrote About the War* (1931), pp.24–5.

This passage was the basis for a widespread belief that Shaw had recommended soldiers to shoot their officers, so that he came to be regarded as a pro-German pacifist traitor.

There was another kind of scepticism. At least one poet tried, even in the opening months, to imagine what it was like to be an ordinary soldier at the Front. W. W. Gibson, one of the leading Georgians and a close friend of Brooke, began writing brief, typically Georgian poems which used simple language and 'realism' to bring home something of the reality of modern war.

> We ate our breakfast lying on our backs
> Because the shells were screeching overhead.
> I bet a rasher to a loaf of bread
> That Hull United would beat Halifax
> When Jimmy Stainthorpe played full-back instead
> Of Billy Bradford. Ginger raised his head
> And cursed, and took the bet, and dropt back dead.
> We ate our breakfast lying on our backs
> Because the shells were screeching overhead.

W. W. Gibson, 'Breakfast', *The Nation* (17 October 1914).

Although 'Breakfast' is not especially realistic or anti-heroic, it has deceived several anthologists into presenting it as work by a disillusioned, trench-hardened soldier-poet. Actually, the poem first appeared in 1914, and Gibson never went near the front. It is worth remembering that a civilian could write like this so early.

War to End War?

Many people who were doubtful about the war at first were attracted by the notion that this was a war to end war: the only way to finish 'Prussianism' was to destroy it by force of arms. This argument was vigorously publicised by H. G. Wells in a series of articles in August, reprinted in September as *The War That Will End War*.

For this is now a war for peace.

It aims straight at disarmament. It aims at a settlement that shall stop this sort of thing for ever. Every soldier who fights against Germany now is a crusader against war. This, the greatest of all wars, is not just another war – it is the last war! England, France, Italy, Belgium, Spain, and all the little countries of Europe, are heartily sick of war; the Tsar has expressed a passionate hatred of war; the most of Asia is unwarlike; the United States has no illusions about war. And never was war begun so joylessly, and never was war begun with so grim a resolution. In England, France, Belgium, Russia, there is no thought of glory.

We know we face unprecedented slaughter and agonies; we know that for neither side will there be easy triumphs or prancing victories. Already, in that warring sea of men, there is famine as well as hideous butchery, and soon there must come disease.

Can it be otherwise?

We face, perhaps, the most awful winter that mankind has ever faced.

But we English and our allies, who did not seek this catastrophe, face it with anger and determination rather than despair.

Through this war we have to march, through pain, through agonies of the spirit worse than pain, through seas of blood and filth. We English have not had things kept from us. We know what war is; we have no delusions. We have read books that tell us of the stench of battlefields, and the nature of wounds, books that Germany suppressed and hid from her people. And we face these horrors to make an end of them.

There shall be no more Kaisers, there shall be no more Krupps [German armaments manufacturers]; we are resolved. That foolery shall end!

And not simply the present belligerents must come into the settlement.

All America, Italy, China, the Scandinavian Powers, must have a voice in the final readjustment, and set their hands to the ultimate guarantees. I do not mean that they need fire a single shot or load a single gun. But they must come in. And in particular to the United States do we look to play a part in that pacification of the world for which our whole nation is working, and for which, by the thousand, men are now laying down their lives.

H. G. Wells, 'Why Britain Went to War', *The War That Will End War* (1914), pp.11–13.

Wells's position was widely shared, even by moderate Socialists and by Liberals who had originally hoped for British neutrality, but he had his critics, notably Bertrand Russell, whose intense opposition to the war never wavered.

Mr Wells writes glibly . . . of 'the war that will end war', and tells us that he is 'enthusiastic for this war against Prussian militarism'. I cannot share his enthusiasm. War will not be ended by a war, or by enthusiasm *'against'* others. War will only end when people so realise its horrors, so guard their reason from the credulities and obsessions of war-fever that they prefer to refrain from fighting even when they have a just cause. We almost unanimously believe we have a just cause, but so does every other nation – not only France, but Russia, Germany, Austria and Japan. To the men of each of these nations it seems that they have taken up arms in defence of the right, and to resist hostile invasion. They cannot all be wholly right; it is very unlikely that any one of them is wholly wrong. In each exists a love of dominion and a fear of aggression: the love of dominion, often silent and unavowed, but sufficient to make each nation believe in the possibility of aggression by another nation like itself. The only road to a secure peace lies through a reform in the thoughts and feelings of common men: an unwillingness to inflict humiliation on others for the sake of one's own triumph, a more calm and equable courage which provides against reasonable risks quietly, without hostile feeling, and without the nightmare terror that makes men rush into the very calamity of which they are in dread.

No war is just except a war to repel actual invasion. If our share in this war were limited to the expulsion of the Germans from Belgium and France, it might be defended as merely resistance to aggression, but Germany is itself being invaded, and at a later stage it is not unlikely that we shall participate in the invasion. Whatever the origin of the war, there is every reason to fear that our Government wishes it to develop into a war of conquest, in which we shall seize German colonies and assist Russia to wreak barbaric vengeance upon the populations of Prussia and Austria. The brutal humiliation of a great and civilised nation is not the road to universal peace; it is the way to perpetuate the old bad hatreds, the brooding thirst for revenge, which have grown out of Prussia's insolent triumph in 1870.

Bertrand Russell, 'Will This War End War?', *The Labour Leader*, 10 September 1914.

Russell's fear that Britain was really embarking on a war of conquest was later to influence Sassoon, and through him Wilfred Owen, but in 1914 most people would have dismissed the idea as absurd; it was not comfortable to recognise too clearly that destroying Prussianism meant destroying the whole fabric of German society and its *Kultur* and that the German colonies were desirable pickings.

At the Front: Retreat and Counter-Attack

The task of ending war by war was much larger than most
people imagined or were allowed to know. The small British
Expeditionary Force (BEF) which crossed the Channel was
the country's only defence, except for the Navy and troops
far away in the colonies; its destruction could not be risked,
so it retreated from Mons with inglorious speed when it met
the German advance. A *Times* despatch from Amiens on 30
August described it as a 'broken' army.

> The British force fell back through Bavai on a front
> between Valenciennes and Maubeuge, then through Le
> Quesnoy, where deep fighting took place, southwards
> continually. Regiments were grievously injured, and
> the broken army fought its way desperately with many
> stands, forced backwards and ever backwards by the
> sheer unconquerable mass of numbers of an enemy
> prepared to throw away three or four men for the life
> of every British soldier. Where it is at present it might
> not be well to say even if I knew, but I do not know,
> though I have seen today in different neighbourhoods
> some units of it. But there are some things which it is
> eminently right that I should say.
>   Tonight I write to the sound of guns. All the
> afternoon the guns were going on the Eastern roads.
> A German aeroplane flew over us, this morning, and
> was brought crashing down.
>   An R.E. chauffeur told me that the axle of his car
> was broken and he had to abandon it. We had no more
> than left it when it also was blown up. In scattered
> units with the enemy ever on its heels the Fourth
> Division, all that was left of 20,000 fine troops,
> streamed southward.
>   Our losses are very great. I have seen the broken
> bits of many regiments. Let me repeat that there is no
> failure in discipline, no panic, no throwing up the
> sponge. Every one's temper is sweet, and nerves do
> not show. A group of men, it may be a dozen, or less
> or more, arrives, under the command of whoever is

entitled to command it. The men are battered with marching, and ought to be weak with hunger, for, of course, no commissariat could cope with such a case, but they are steady and cheerful, and wherever they arrive make straight for the proper authority, report themselves, and seek news of their regiment.

I saw two men give such reports after saluting smartly. 'Very badly cut up, Sir,' was the phrase one used of his regiment. The other said, 'Very heavy loss, I'm afraid, Sir,' when asked if much was left. . . .

The German commanders in the north advance their men as if they had an inexhaustible supply. Of the bravery of the men it is not necessary to speak. . . . Last week, so great was their superiority in numbers that they could no more be stopped than the waves of the sea. Their shrapnel is markedly bad, though their gunners are excellent at finding the range. On the other hand, their machine guns are of the most deadly efficacy, and are very numerous. Their rifle shooting is described as not first-class, but their numbers bring on the infantry till frequently they and the Allied troops meet finally in bayonet tussles. Superiority of numbers in men and guns, especially in machine guns; a most successfully organised system of scouting by aeroplanes and Zeppelins; motors carrying machine guns; cavalry; and extreme mobility are elements of their present success.

To sum up, the first great German effort has succeeded. We have to face the fact that the British Expeditionary Force, which bore the great weight of the blow, has suffered terrible losses and requires immediate and immense reinforcement. The British Expeditionary Force has won indeed imperishable glory, but it needs men, men, and yet more men.

Despatch from 'Our Special Correspondent'
Amiens, *The Times*, 30 August
1914.

Although this uniquely honest report produced a surge in

recruiting, the military authorities were horrified and soon the only journalists allowed near the front were a handful of selected, uniformed and rigidly censored 'War Correspondents'. (In the later stages of the war, the fighting troops were sickened by newspaper reporting; they were unaware that the cheery news from the front which they found so objectionable had often been fed to Fleet Street by their own commanders.) The desperate need for more men had to be advertised without risking damage to public confidence.

The first months of the war were a period of rapid military movements, as the German thrust into France lost its impetus and was forced back by the French from the environs of Paris. The BEF managed to recover from the retreat and to put up a strong resistance in Flanders. The outcome was uncertain for many weeks. In late October the line seemed about to collapse, but on the 31st the Worcestershire Regiment counter-attacked at the village of Gheluvelt and brought the enemy to a halt. From then on the British established themselves in that area, outside the medieval city of Ypres, and were to hold the Ypres 'Salient' until the end of the war (Plates 4 and 5). The fight by the Worcesters was considered at the time to have saved the Army and the nation, although it was on a small scale compared to later engagements. It is recorded in the unemotional words of the official historian.

> One company of the Worcestershire had been sent up earlier in the day to support the right of the 1st (Guards) Brigade. Thus, when the battalion was given the signal to advance south-eastwards, the actual strength of the three companies present was only 7 officers and 350 other ranks. The XLI. Brigade R.F.A. was detailed to support them, and from the south-west corner of Polygon Wood, where he had his observing post on the roof of a cottage, Lieut.-Colonel S. Lushington, commanding it, could see the whole advance. For the first six hundred yards of the movement the Worcestershire were under cover of woods on their left, defiladed from view, though not protected from fire, and moved in fours. On reaching a small belt of trees west of Polderhoek Chateau,

Major Hankey deployed the battalion into two lines
at fifty yards distance, with two companies in the first
line, a small party under an o' ̄ ̣ẹ̣r being specially
detailed to secure the exposed rigḥt flank. There were
still a thousand yards to traverse, and the scene
that confronted the Worcestershire was sufficient to
demoralize the strongest nerves and shake the finest
courage. The stretch of country which they saw in
front of them was devoid of cover of any kind; beyond
it lay the fences and enclosures of Gheluvelt Chateau
and village, in which many houses were in flames.
Wounded and stragglers in considerable numbers were
making their way back to the shelter of the woods,
some of whom cried as the advancing troops passed
through them, that to go on was certain death, whilst
the enemy's high explosive and shrapnel bursting
overhead gave point and substance to the warning.
But, nothing daunted, the three companies swept on.
The first two hundred yards were crossed in one long
rush; nevertheless, the Worcestershire were observed
by the enemy's artillery directly they appeared in sight,
and its fire was redoubled. Over a hundred men fell,
but the rest still pressed on. The wire fences of the
enclosures near the village and the wall and railing of
the chateau grounds were reached and passed, and
contact with the enemy's infantry gained. The Bavari-
ans (*16th Reserve Infantry Regiment*) and other Germans north of the Menin road, and actually in rear of
part of the South Wales Borderers, were enjoying the
repose of victory, searching for water and looting, and
in no expectation of such an onslaught. They offered
no organized resistance, and were soon fleeing back
in confusion through the village. The Worcestershire
pushed on until they reached what remained of the
South Wales Borderers and Scots Guards, who, almost
surrounded, were still holding their own on the south-
west face of the chateau grounds. Major Hankey
established his three companies on their right in the
sunken road which leads from the chateau to the
village, with the outer flank at the corner where this
road turns south-east.

General FitzClarence, who had accompanied Major Hankey to the place of deployment and remained there to watch the counter-attack, on seeing its success galloped back to Polygon Wood and reported to the 1st Division:– "It's all right, my line still holds north of the village".

The position of the Worcestershire in the sunken road was by no means comfortable; they received a considerable amount of machine-gun and rifle fire from Gheluvelt, so patrols were sent in to settle with the enemy. They found there and drove out a few German patrols and scouts – who dodged about as if bewildered and fired at random – and took a few prisoners. The bulk of the invaders seem to have fled when the counter-attack reached the chateau grounds.

The greater part of the village was again in possession of the British, but still by no means secured; and at 3.45 p.m. Major Hankey sent an order to his fourth company, which since morning had been entrenched behind the light railway about four hundred yards north-west of the village, to come up into line with the remainder of the battalion. This it did at once and extended through the village to the church and churchyard; but, being unable to get in touch with any troops on its right, turned back its flank. It also sent patrols into the rest of the village, which was burning in several places and was being shelled by the artillery of both sides. The patrols reached the cross roads at the south-eastern exit; but, although they had suspicions that there were Germans in the scattered houses beyond, they were not fired on. Gheluvelt was definitely in British hands.

> J. E. Edmonds, *History of the Great War. Based on Official Documents: Military Operations, France and Belgium, 1914*, vol.2 (1925), pp.328–9.

Robert Bridges, the Poet Laureate, celebrated this event in a classical epitaph.

Askest thou of these graves? They'll tell thee, O
stranger, in England
How we Worcesters lie where we redeem'd the
battle.

Robert Bridges, 'Gheluvelt', *October and Other
Poems* (1920).

The Nation's Duty

A successful war effort needs strong moral reinforcement.
Like the other belligerent peoples, the British were confident
that they were on the side of religion and honour against a
ruthless, evil enemy. Among the many churchmen who
supported the recruiting drive, none was more enthusiastic
and effective than the Bishop of London, A. F. Winnington
Ingram. On 31 August, for example, the Bishop climbed onto
a wagon at a Territorial camp and preached to five thousand
men.

> Just think of it, to have your children and your
> grandchildren speak of you as the man who fought at
> the second Battle of Waterloo! There has been going
> on this week the beginning of what will be the most
> famous battle of the modern world, one that will ring
> on beyond the fame of Waterloo; and you have your
> chance to take your part in it.
> It has been said, "It is a glorious thing to be alive in
> the world to-day," and I say to you, It is a glorious
> thing for *you* to be alive to-day.
> What, then, are the motives that should be stirring
> you up to show your best mettle? I have mentioned
> one of them – to support all that England stands for,
> and to repay all you owe to England. I will mention
> another, what our ancestors did in the past for the
> country which they loved. I read the other day what
> I thought some very stirring words. They may appeal
> to some of you:

Here lies a clerk who half his life had spent
Toiling at ledgers in a city grey,
Thinking that so his days would drift away
With no lance broken in life's tournament:
But ever 'twixt the books and his bright eyes
The gleaming eagles of the legions came,
And horsemen charging under phantom skies
Went thundering past beneath the oriflamme.

And now these waiting dreams are satisfied,
For in the end he heard the bugle call,
And to his country then he gave his all,
When in the first high hour of life he died;
And falling thus, he wants no recompense
Who found his battle in the last resort;
Nor needs he any hearse to bear him hence
Who goes to join the men of Agincourt.

The men of Agincourt – ay, and of Creçy, and
Inkermann, and Alma, and Waterloo, the spirits of
those who died for their country on those glorious
fields – are with us to-day to inspire us to show that
we are true descendants of the men who fought there.
Are we going to fight at this crisis of our country's
history less bravely than they fought? Never!

> A. F. Winnington Ingram, 'A Call to Arms', *A
> Day of God* (1914), pp.20–1.

The sermon from which this extract comes was said to have
raised six regular battalions. The poem quoted by the Bishop
is 'The Volunteer' by Herbert Asquith, a son of the Prime
Minister; first published on 8 August, it had actually been
written a year or more earlier, but it suited the new mood
and soon became well known.

Clearly, literature could contribute to the nation's morale
and to the recruiting campaign. Writers agreed that the
response to Germany had to be moral and cultural, not just
military; as *The Times* pointed out, Germany was not driven
by mere greed and self-interest, despite some British assertions
to the contrary.

Germany is proving now that Mr Norman Angell's great illusion is not the illusion that really produces war. It is not a mistaken notion of self-interest that has made Germany consent joyfully to this war, but a wrong moral idea. War to Treitschke and General Bernhardi and all the conscious and unconscious followers of Nietzsche is noble and splendid in itself; a German war is something to be proud of, like German music, not only for the heroism that may be shown in it, but as an achievement of the German people.

The Times, Fourth Leader, 2 September 1914.

On the same day the paper printed a letter from Robert Bridges and a poem by Kipling. Bridges was in no doubt about the nature of the war.

Since the beginning of this war the meaning of it has in one respect considerably changed, and I hope that our people will see that it is primarily a holy war. It is manifestly a war between Christ and the Devil. . . . The infernal machine which has been scientifically preparing for the last twenty-five years is now on its wild career like one of Mr Wells's inventions, and wherever it goes it will leave desolation behind it and put all material progress back for at least half a century. There was never anything in the world worthier of extermination, and it is the plain duty of civilised nations to unite to drive it back into its home and exterminate it there.

Robert Bridges, letter, *The Times*, 2 September 1914.

Kipling's poem was equally uncompromising but more pagan, although the Bishop of London was often to quote it.

For all we have and are,
For all our children's fate,
Stand up and take the war,
The Hun is at the gate!

Our world has passed away,
In wantonness o'erthrown.
There is nothing left to-day
But steel and fire and stone!
    Though all we knew depart,
    The old Commandments stand:–
    'In courage keep your heart,
    In strength lift up your hand.'

Once more we hear the word
That sickened earth of old:–
'No law except the Sword
Unsheathed and uncontrolled.'
Once more it knits mankind,
Once more the nations go
To meet and break and bind
A crazed and driven foe.

Comfort, content, delight,
The ages' slow-bought gain,
They shrivelled in a night.
Only ourselves remain
To face the naked days
In silent fortitude,
Through perils and dismays
Renewed and re-renewed.
    Though all we made depart,
    The old Commandments stand:–
    'In patience keep your heart,
    In strength lift up your hand.'

No easy hopes or lies
Shall bring us to our goal,
But iron sacrifice
Of body, will, and soul.

There is but one task for all–
One life for each to give.
Who stands if Freedom fall?
Who dies if England live?

> Rudyard Kipling, 'For all we have and are', *The Times*, 2 September 1914.

These three statements in *The Times* of 2 September must have been in the minds of the twenty or more distinguished writers who assembled that day for a secret conference at the new propaganda department in London to discuss how they could use their talents in the service of the nation. Among the immediate results of this meeting were Hardy's famous recruiting poem, 'The Song of the Soldiers' or 'Men Who March Away' (*The Times*, 9 September) and a long public statement by 52 authors.

> The undersigned writers, comprising amongst them men and women of the most divergent political and social views, some of them having been for years ardent champions of good will towards Germany, and many of them extreme advocates of peace, are nevertheless agreed that Great Britain could not without dishonour have refused to take part in the present war. . . .
> When Belgium in her dire need appealed to Great Britain to carry out her pledge this country's course was clear. She had either to break faith, letting the sanctity of treaties and the rights of small nations count for nothing before the threat of naked force, or she had to fight. She did not hesitate, and we trust she will not lay down arms till Belgium's integrity is restored and her wrongs redressed. . . .
> We observe that various German apologists, official and semi-official, admit that their country has been false to its pledged word, and dwell almost with pride on the 'frightfulness' of the examples by which it has sought to spread terror in Belgium, but they excuse all these proceedings by a strange and novel plea.

German culture and civilisation are so superior to those of other nations that all steps taken to assert them are more than justified; and the destiny of Germany to be the dominating force in Europe and the world is so manifest that ordinary rules of morality do not hold good in her case, but actions are good or bad simply as they help or hinder the accomplishment of that destiny.

These views, inculcated upon the present generation of Germans by many celebrated historians and teachers, seem to us both dangerous and insane. . . .

Whatever the world-destiny of Germany may be, we in Great Britain are ourselves conscious of a destiny and a duty. That destiny and duty, alike for us and for all the English-speaking race, call upon us to uphold the rule of common justice between civilised peoples, to defend the rights of small nations, and to maintain the free and law-abiding ideals of Western Europe against the rule of 'Blood and Iron' and the domination of the whole Continent by a military caste.

For these reasons and others the undersigned feel bound to support the cause of the Allies with all their strength, with a full conviction of its righteousness, and with a deep sense of its vital import to the future of the world.

'Britain's Destiny and Duty/Declaration by Authors', *The Times*, 18 September 1914.

The 52 signatories included J. M. Barrie, Arnold Bennett, Laurence Binyon (whose 'For the Fallen' appeared in *The Times* on 21 September), Bridges, G. K. Chesterton, Conan Doyle, Galsworthy, Rider Haggard, Hardy, Kipling, Masefield, Newbolt and Wells. Many of them were to publish articles, poems, books or plays in support of the Allied cause in the next few years. The propaganda authorities, who included several authors (notably John Buchan in 1917 and Bennett in 1918), gave assistance but kept well out of sight. Authors were sent to America to lecture, although Kipling was not allowed to go because his views were considered too extreme. Bennett, Doyle, Shaw, Wells, Masefield, Hilaire Belloc and others were sent to France and encouraged to write about what little they had been allowed to see. A scheme got under way in 1916 to send out numerous 'War Artists', who in due course produced the impressive collection of paintings and drawings now in the Imperial War Museum; on the whole, the artists did better work than the authors, but that may be because they were given much more time and freedom near the line.

A principal target for British propaganda was opinion in neutral America (hence the 52 authors' reference to 'the English-speaking race'). Modern readers of 1914–16 speeches and publications need to keep this fact in mind. British writers were often not primarily trying to persuade their own people, although they were advised not to address the United States too directly. When leading politicians spoke at a rally in September, they were aiming at the Empire and, beyond it, at the United States and all neutral countries. The Prime Minister defended the decision to go to war, stressing alleged atrocities in Belgium and the recent burning of medieval Louvain, two topics that had aroused international horror.

> But let me ask you, and through you the world outside, what would have been our condition as a nation to-day if through timidity, or through a perverted calculation of self-interest, or through a paralysis of the sense of honour and duty, we had been base enough to be false to our word and faithless to our friends? Our eyes would have been turned at this moment, with those of the whole civilised world, to Belgium, a small State which has lived for more than seventy years under a several and collective guarantee to which we, in common with Prussia and Austria, were parties; and we should have seen at the instance and by the action of two of those guaranteeing Powers, her neutrality violated, her independence strangled, her territory made use of as affording the easiest and most convenient road to a war of unprovoked aggression against France. We, the British people, should at this moment have been standing by with

folded arms and with such countenance as we could command, while this small and unprotected State, in defence of her vital liberties, made a heroic stand against overweening and overwhelming forces. We should have been admiring as detached spectators the siege of Liège, the steady and manful resistance of the small army, the occupation of her capital with its splendid traditions and memories, the gradual forcing back of the patriotic defenders of their native land to the ramparts of Antwerp, countless outrages suffered by them, buccaneering levies exacted from the unoffending civil population, and, finally, the greatest crime committed against civilisation and culture since the Thirty Years' War – the sack of Louvain, with its buildings, its pictures, its unique library, its unrivalled associations, the shameless holocaust of irreparable treasures lit up by blind barbarian vengeance.

What account could we, the Government and the people of this country, have been able to render to the tribunal of our national conscience and sense of honour if, in defiance of our plighted and solemn obligations, we had endured and had not done our best to prevent – yes, to avenge – these intolerable wrongs?

For my part, I say that sooner than be a silent witness, which means, in effect, a willing accomplice to this tragic triumph of force over law and of brutality over freedom, I would see this country of ours blotted out of the pages of history.

H. H. Asquith, speech at Guildhall, London, 4 September 1914, quoted in *Through Terror to Triumph* (1914), pp.56–7.

US and German Responses

The British and Allied cause did not carry conviction everywhere. Although many Americans were sympathetic, some, especially those of German descent, had long regarded the

British Empire as the great enemy of freedom. France was suspect as a source of revolution and Czarist Russia was the epitome of autocratic cruelty. To one American poet the Kaiser was the 'Prince of Peace'.

> May thy victorious armies rout
>   The yellow hordes against thee hurled,
> The Czar whose sceptre is the knout,
>   And France, the harlot of the world!
>
> But thy great task will not be done
>   Until thou vanquish utterly
> The Norman sister of the Hun,
>   England, the Serpent of the Sea.
>
> The flame of war her tradesmen fanned
>   Shall yet consume her, fleet and field:
> The star of Frederick guide thy hand,
>   The God of Bismarck be thy shield!
>
> Against the fell Barbarian horde
>   Thy people stand, a living wall;
> Now fight for God's peace with thy sword,
>   For if thou fail, a world shall fall!
>
> G. S. Viereck, 'Wilhelm II, Prince of Peace',
Songs of Armageddon (1916).

In Germany itself, Britain's declaration of war was held to be an act of the utmost treachery. When the Fatherland had been in mortal danger, trapped between the rapidly mobilising powers of France and Russia, and had taken to arms in self-defence, the British had thrown aside their sham neutrality, greedily hoping for a chance to seize German colonies and trading interests. This line of argument bewildered most British people, although it was intelligible enough to critics of the war such as Shaw and Russell. Readers of *The Times* on 29 October were astonished to read some verses which had recently appeared in a Munich weekly.

French and Russian they matter not,
A blow for a blow and a shot for a shot:
We love them not, we hate them not,
We hold the Weichsel and Vosges gate,
We have but one and only hate,
We love as one, we hate as one,
We have one foe and one alone.

He is known to you all, he is known to you all,
He crouches behind the dark grey flood,
Full of envy, of rage, of craft, of gall,
Cut off by waves that are thicker than blood.
Come, let us stand at the Judgement place,
An oath to swear to, face to face,
An oath of bronze no wind can shake,
An oath for our sons and their sons to take.
Come, hear the word, repeat the word,
Throughout the Fatherland make it heard.
We will never forgo our hate,
We have all but a single hate,
We love as one, we hate as one,
We have one foe, and one alone –
ENGLAND!

> Ernst Lissauer, 'Hymn of Hate', translation in
> British, American and other newspapers,
> Autumn 1914, st.1–2.

Whatever Lissauer's verses may have done for German morale (some Germans deplored them), they were a gift to British propagandists and were given extensive publicity. The word 'hate' passed into the wartime vocabulary, men in the trenches adopting it as a humorous term for German shelling. German protestations of innocence were treated with contempt, British commentators pointing to pre-war 'Prussianism' and the invasion of Belgium as proof of guilt (Plate 1).

The Trenches

The trench line had become established in October 1914. Modern firepower and railways made defence easier than attack. The line was held by troops from many nations; on the Allied side, the French sector was much longer than the British, which ran for a comparatively short distance through northern France and part of Belgium. The Germans, being the invaders, with the industries of northern France now under their control, could afford to set up long-term, heavily fortified positions, but the Allies had to think of advancing, and their shallow trenches were to cost them dear in 1916 and later. Frank Richards, who was to survive many battles and serve for a time under Sassoon and Graves, remembered 'digging in' for the first time. Trenches were always constructed on a dog-leg pattern, with alternating forward 'bays' and rear 'traverses', but the early versions were dangerously inadequate.

Little did we think when we were digging those trenches that we were digging our future homes; but they were the beginnings of the long stretch that soon went all the way from the North Sea to Switzerland and they were our homes for the next four years. Each platoon dug in on its own, with gaps of about forty yards between each platoon. B Company were in support, but one platoon of B were on the extreme right of the Battalion's front line. On our left were the 1st Middlesex, and on our right was a battalion of Indian native infantry. Our Company Commander used to visit the other three platoons at night; he, the Second-in-Command of the Company and the platoon officer stayed on the extreme right of our trench. We dug those trenches simply for fighting; they were breast-high with the front parapet on ground level and in each bay we stood shoulder to shoulder. We were so squeezed for room that whenever an officer passed along the trench one man would get behind the traverse if the officer wanted to stay awhile in that bay. No man was allowed to fire from behind the traverse:

because the least deflection of his rifle would put a bullet through someone in the bay in front of him. Traverses were made to counteract enfilade rifle-fire. Sandbags were unknown at this time.

A part of our trench crossed a willow ditch and about forty yards in front of us we blocked this ditch with a little bank which was to be our listening post at night. The ditch was dry at present. Every order was passed up the trench by word of mouth, and we found in many instances that by the time an order reached the last man it was entirely different from what the first man had passed along. When our Company Commander passed along the trench we had to squeeze our bodies into the front parapet to allow him to pass. If a man did not move smart enough, out would come his revolver and he would threaten to blow the man's ruddy brains out.

Frank Richards, *Old Soldiers Never Die* (1933), pp.34–5.

Soon trenches became more spacious and efficient. A whole way of life gradually evolved in response to the new conditions. Richards described his sector as it was later in 1914.

Our trenches were flooded. We were knee-deep in some places, and it was continually raining; but we had hand-pumps which we had scrounged from Houplines and worked them day and night. At night, we numbered off, one, two, three, one, two, three – ones up on sentry, twos and threes working. Every evening at twilight the order would come "Stand to!" and every man in the trench would get up on the fire-step and gaze across no-man's-land at the enemy's trench. The same thing would happen at dawn in the morning. After standing to about five minutes the order would come "Stand down!" A sentry would be on from stand to in the evening until stand to the next morning, which during the long winter nights meant fourteen or fifteen hours continual standing on the fire-step and staring out at no-man's-land. At night all sentries stood head and shoulders above the parapet: they could see better and were less liable to be surprised. Also when enemy machine-guns were traversing or enemy sentries firing it was better to be hit through the chest and shoulders than through the head; although that was all according to a man's luck. Twos and threes were working all night, some carrying R.E. material from Houplines – this consisted of duckboards for laying on the bottom of the trench when the water was cleared out, barbed wire, sandbags and other material for building trenches. Some were carrying rations, others filling sandbags. There was a great dump of sand just behind our trench on the river bank which came in very useful. Some were putting out barbed wire in front, and others strengthening the parapet. A good standing trench was about six foot six deep, so that a man could walk upright during the day in safety from rifle-fire. In each bay of the trench we constructed fire-steps about two feet higher than the bottom of the trench, which enabled us to stand head and shoulders above the parapet. During the day we were working in reliefs, and we would snatch an hour's sleep, when we could, on a wet and muddy fire-step, wet through to the skin ourselves.

Ibid., pp.58–9.

Heavy shelling could undo months of digging and make repairs impossible, as a Guards Captain recorded six months later.

The trenches which the battalion was holding were new to us, and were very lively; and the contrast between the peaceful life I was leading with you and the children last Wednesday and my occupation the following day and night could scarcely have been greater. Nowhere along the whole front are the Germans and ourselves more close together than there. Twelve to fifteen yards was all that separated us in the advanced portions of the trench, and the ground between was a shapeless waste – a mass of mine-craters, including two so large that they are known officially as Etna and Vesuvius.

The ragged aspect of this advanced trench I cannot picture to you. The hundreds of bombs which explode in and around it each day and night have reduced it to a state of wild dilapidation that is indescribable. There is not a sandbag that is not torn to shreds, and the trench itself is half filled by the earth and debris that have dribbled down. So shallow and emaciated has this bit of trench now become that you have to stoop low or your head and shoulders poke above the parapet, and so near are you to the enemy that you have to move in perfect silence. The slightest visible movement brings a hail of bullets from the snipers, and the slightest sound a storm of hand-grenades.

The conditions are such that you cannot repair the damages as they should be repaired. You just have to do the best you can, with the result that when the tide of war has passed beyond these blood-soaked lines they will soon become obliterated and lost among the wilderness of craters. The tripper who will follow will pass them by, and will no doubt pour out his sentiment on the more arresting concrete dug-outs and the well-planned earthworks of the reserve lines well behind.

Rowland Feilding, *War Letters to a Wife* (1929),
pp.29–30.

Despite the chaos and horrors, British writers were to look back on the early stages of trench warfare with a little nostalgia. Comradeship was strong. The amateurishness of everything had a certain charm, especially when one could think of the conscripted troops on the other side as slaves of a ruthless tyranny. At the end of 1914 came the unofficial 'Christmas truce', when British and Germans fraternised in No Man's Land, an event which has often been misunderstood. The troops on both sides took the chance to strengthen their parapets. Personal friendliness between soldiers did not mean a loss of the will to fight; as far as the average 'Tommy' was concerned, the war was against the Kaiser and German aggression, not against 'Jerry' as an individual. And sometimes, even by soldiers, the enemy was referred to as 'the Hun' or 'frightful Fritz', terms taken from the Kaiser himself, who had once urged his troops to be like the Huns in using 'a certain frightfulness' against their opponents; the executions of Belgian civilians were regarded as evidence of a deliberate policy of 'frightfulness' (see, for example, the statement by 52 authors, p.55 above).

'Hate'

British public opinion regarded submarine and air warfare, neither of which had been experienced before, as further evidence of German barbarism. The outrage when the first merchant ships were torpedoed, and when coastal towns were bombed or shelled, seems naive today, but it grew louder in the spring of 1915 when London suffered its first Zeppelin raids and a civilian liner, the *Lusitania*, was sunk in the Atlantic with American as well as British casualties. Bernard Shaw pointed out that protests – he called them 'squealing' – at attacks on civilian targets revealed precisely the terror and panic that the enemy wished to arouse, but the public, which had been so idealistic in 1914, was beginning to want revenge. There were anti-German riots in May. As a result of public pressure 'aliens' were interned 'for their own safety', doomed to spend the rest of the war in prison camps because they were of foreign descent and might be spies. The Lord Chancellor, Haldane, was driven out of office, unjustly branded as a German sympathiser. The Headmaster of Eton was condemned for suggesting that in the end the German people would have to be lived with as neighbours and fellow humans. Anti-German hysteria was becoming endemic in Britain, ready to flare up whenever the newspapers chose to fuel it. Soldiers were little better than civilians. When meetings of 'cranks' (pacifists) were broken up, soldiers were often at the head of the mob. Servicemen seem to have been among the most devoted readers of that viciously anti-German newspaper, *John Bull*, and its unscrupulous editor, Horatio

Bottomley, the self-styled 'servant of the soldier'.

The word for all this is Lissauer's: hate. Hate is perhaps an essential element in war, when each side has to persuade itself that the enemy is fit to be killed in large numbers. The ground had been prepared in Britain by decades of fear and dislike of the new Germany. Appeals for calm and tolerance had small chance of being heard. Even in 1914 the critic and moralist Arthur Clutton-Brock felt it urgently necessary to point out that the Germans were as human as anybody else.

> These hosts are not inhuman, whatever evil design has ranged them against us, but men like ourselves to whom we also seem inhuman hosts; and if some voice from heaven could suddenly speak the truth to us the weapons would drop from our hands and we should laugh in each other's faces until we wept to think of all the dead that could not share the truth with us, and the wounded who could not be cured by it, and the widows and orphans to whom it could not give back their husbands and fathers. For the truth, the ultimate truth, behind all arguments and national conflicts and all the pride of victory and the shame of defeat, is that we are men in whom the spirit is stronger than the flesh, in whom the spirit desires love more than the flesh desires hatred. We have a strange way of showing that now; but, whatever our own delusions, each nation knows that it is fighting the delusions of the other; and against them it is necessary for us to fight as if against the hallucinated fury of a madman. Yet the fighting is best done as good soldiers do it who know that their enemies are men, not devils, and who fear them the less because they do not hate.
>
> A little time ago a French paper praised us for our quiet English pride, as being different from the nervous and bloated pride of the Germans. Well, it may be better-mannered, because we are more used to power than they are; but we shall do well not to be proud of the quality of our pride, and not to rely on it to keep us calm and steadfast and humane. There are times when pride must be appealed to before it will master

the lower passions, but humility is always on its guard against them. Pride makes comparisons with other men or other nations – we will not behave as they do because we are Englishmen – but humility compares us with what we should like to be; it never flatters us to make us good. If now we are to set a standard of behaviour before ourselves, let us imagine the historian of a distant and happier future looking back upon us with full knowledge and judging our conduct and our temper in this time. We should wish him to say of us that we waged war, not only resolutely and successfully, but with a spirit new to the world; and that, because of that spirit, there came a new kindness and wisdom. . . .

A. Clutton-Brock, 'The Illusions of War',
Thoughts on the War (1914), pp.74–5.

The future historian cannot be so generous. Despite their many admirable qualities, most people in wartime Britain seem to have developed hatred for their enemy by early 1915. Kipling saw the change and grimly approved it.

It was not part of their blood,
    It came to them very late
With long arrears to make good,
    When the English began to hate.

They were not easily moved,
    They were icy willing to wait
Till every count should be proved,
    Ere the English began to hate.

Their voices were even and low,
    Their eyes were level and straight.
There was neither sign nor show,
    When the English began to hate.

It was not preached to the crowd,
    It was not taught by the State.
No man spoke it aloud,
    When the English began to hate.

It was not suddenly bred,
    It will not swiftly abate,
Through the chill years ahead,
    When Time shall count from the date
    That the English began to hate.

Rudyard Kipling, 'The Beginnings', A Diversity
of Creatures (1917).

In *A Diversity of Creatures*, this poem follows a short story, 'Mary Postgate', which Kipling wrote in March 1915. Mary Postgate is a spinster 'companion' to an elderly lady, Miss Fowler, whose disagreeable nephew, Wynn, is killed early in the war. Mary, who had been secretly attracted to Wynn, takes it upon herself to burn his possessions. When the bonfire is alight, she goes into the village and sees a child who had been killed in a sudden air-raid. Returning to the garden, she finds the German pilot lying badly injured, entangled in his parachute. Spurning his entreaties for help, she attends to the fire.

The exercise of stoking had given her a glow which seemed to reach to the marrow of her bones. She hummed – Mary never had a voice – to herself. She had never believed in all those advanced views – though Miss Fowler herself leaned a little that way – of woman's work in the world; but now she saw there was much to be said for them. This, for instance, was *her* work – work which no man, least of all Dr. Hennis, would ever have done. A man, at such a crisis, would be what Wynn called a 'sportsman'; would leave everything to fetch help, and would certainly bring it into the house. Now a woman's business was to make a happy home for – for a husband and children. Failing these – it was not a thing one should allow one's mind to dwell upon – but—
    'Stop it!' Mary cried once more across the shadows. 'Nein, I tell you! Ich haben der todt Kinder gesehn.'
    But it was a fact. A woman who had missed these things could still be useful – more useful than a man

in certain respects. She thumped like a pavior through the settling ashes at the secret thrill of it. The rain was damping the fire, but she could feel – it was too dark to see – that her work was done. There was a dull red glow at the bottom of the destructor, not enough to char the wooden lid if she slipped it half over against the driving wet. This arranged, she leaned on the poker and waited, while an increasing rapture laid hold on her. She ceased to think. She gave herself up to feel. Her long pleasure was broken by a sound that she had waited for in agony several times in her life. She leaned forward and listened, smiling. There could be no mistake. She closed her eyes and drank it in. Once it ceased abruptly.

'Go on,' she murmured, half aloud. 'That isn't the end.'

Then the end came very distinctly in a lull between two rain-gusts. Mary Postgate drew her breath short between her teeth and shivered from head to foot. '*That's* all right,' said she contentedly, and went up to the house, where she scandalised the whole routine by taking a luxurious hot bath before tea, and came down looking, as Miss Fowler said when she saw her lying all relaxed on the other sofa, 'quite handsome!'

> Rudyard Kipling, 'Mary Postgate' (first published September 1915).

This unnerving story is as outspoken in its psychological insights as Lawrence's 'The Prussian Officer'. Perhaps the strains of war were hastening the discovery and description of mental processes which had hitherto been largely out of bounds to novelists.

Heroism

Talk of heroism increased. The costly battle of Neuve Chapelle in March 1915 left long casualty lists. The spiritual nature of the war received more emphasis than ever. In April *The Times* reported the Easter Sunday service at St Paul's.

> Dean Inge preached . . . He was suffering from
> a severe cold, and his sermon was rather brief in
> consequence. When the Dean entered the pulpit a man
> in the congregation rose to his feet and began a loud
> harangue protesting against the war. He was quickly
> conducted outside the Cathedral.
> The Dean took his text from Isaiah xxvi, v.19:–
> 'Thy dead shall live; my dead bodies shall arise. Awake
> and sing, ye that dwell in the dust, for thy dew is as
> the dew of lights, and the earth shall cast forth the
> dead.'
> There were thousands of English parents, and young
> widows, and young orphans, who on this Easter Day
> were thinking of the hastily made graves in a foreign
> land, where their dearest are sleeping. When the day
> of peace and restored safety dawned for England, as
> please God it would before very long, what of them?
> Would they be left out of it? Was their day over and
> done, while the struggle was still undecided and the
> victory uncertain? How could God refuse them the
> happiness they so well earned, of sharing in our
> rejoicings over the peace?
> He had just read a beautiful little poem on this
> subject, a sonnet by a young writer who would, he
> ventured to think, take rank with our great poets – so
> potent was a time of trouble to evoke genius which
> might otherwise have slumbered. A young soldier
> spoke thus:–

> If I should die, think only this of me:
>   That there's some corner of a foreign field
> That is for ever England. There shall be
>   In that rich earth a richer dust concealed;
> A dust whom England bore, shaped, made aware,
>   Gave, once, her flowers to love, her ways to roam,
> A body of England's, breathing English air,
>   Washed by the rivers, blest by suns of home.

And think, this heart, all evil shed away,
A pulse in the eternal mind, no less
  Gives somewhere back the thoughts by England
  given;
Her sights and sounds; dreams happy as her day;
And laughter, learnt of friends; and gentleness,
  In hearts at peace, under an English heaven.

The enthusiasm of a pure and elevated patriotism, free from hate, bitterness, and fear, had never found a nobler expression. And yet it fell somewhat short of Isaiah's vision and still more of the Christian hope. It was a worthy thought that the dust out of which the happy warrior's body was once compacted was consecrated for ever by the cause for which he died. Yet was there not a tinge of materialism in such an idea? The spirit of heroism and self-sacrifice knew no restrictions of this kind. When it had once shown itself in action, it became part of the whole world's spiritual wealth. The earth was a better place because such things had been done in it. The spirit of the martyr-patriot was everywhere near, where there was a man to say, 'This is how I should like to live and die'. And a Christian would hardly be quite content to think of the brave man's soul as living on only as 'a pulse in the eternal mind'. The Christian hope of immortality was not impersonal.

'Dean Inge at St Paul's/Spirit of the Martyr-
Patriot', *The Times*, 5 April 1915.

Far away in the Aegean Rupert Brooke was already dying of blood poisoning when he was told that his sonnet, 'The Soldier' (originally entitled 'The Recruit'), had been quoted from the pulpit of St Paul's, but he managed to remark with characteristic humour that he was sorry the Dean did not think him quite as good as Isaiah. He had written his five war sonnets during the previous winter, inspired by the refugees and destruction he had seen during the brief fight for Antwerp. Although he was by nature a sceptic and rebel, Antwerp convinced him that the war was in a just cause. The sonnets and subsequent myth-making have resulted in his being remembered as a conventional upper-class patriot. He was actually a middle-class academic and a Fabian Socialist, but it was the heroic image presented by the sonnets – and made famous by Inge's sermon, Brooke's death on St George's Day (23 April) and Churchill's subsequent obituary – which established him as spokesman for all that seemed noblest in the younger generation. That image also left him vulnerable to later criticism; none of the 1914–18 poets has attracted more hostile comment than Brooke, although he is still probably the most famous of them.

There were to be more hero poets, none rivalling Brooke's posthumous influence. In May Julian Grenfell was killed and his 'Into Battle' was printed in *The Times*. October brought the death of Charles Sorley, whose verse has always been regarded as amongst the coolest and most intelligent soldier poetry of the war.

> You are blind like us. Your hurt no man designed,
> And no man claimed the conquest of your land.
> But gropers both through fields of thought confined
> We stumble and we do not understand.
> You only saw your future bigly planned,
> And we, the tapering paths of our own mind,
> And in each other's dearest ways we stand,
> And hiss and hate. And the blind fight the blind.
>
> When it is peace, then we may view again
> With new-won eyes each other's truer form
> And wonder. Grown more loving-kind and warm
> We'll grasp firm hands and laugh at the old pain,
> When it is peace. But until peace, the storm
> The darkness and the thunder and the rain.

> Charles Sorley, 'To Germany', *Marlborough and Other Poems* (1916).

Sorley's verse won the admiration of other young poets, notably Robert Graves and Siegfried Sassoon.

Most of the war's many heroes and heroines, once household names, are now forgotten. One who is still remembered is Nurse Edith Cavell, who was shot by the Germans in October 1915 for assisting Allied soldiers to escape from Belgium. Her death was another bonus for British propaganda; it was said that the event brought in some 40 000 recruits. A devout Christian, Nurse Cavell held to higher values than hate or patriotism. Like Captain Scott, she left a message to the world: 'This I would say, standing as I now do in view of God and Eternity, I realise that patriotism is not enough. I must have no hatred or bitterness towards anyone.'

War service was generally believed to bring out an individual's noblest qualities. A young subaltern signing himself 'A Student in Arms' expounded the religious nature of soldierly virtues in a series of articles in *The Spectator* in late 1915 and early 1916. The 'Student' (Second-Lieutenant Donald Hankey, later killed in action on the Somme) found a large and admiring readership for his studies of the British fighting man. In 'The Beloved Captain' he portrayed the ideal, Christlike officer.

> He was good to look on. He was big and tall, and held himself upright. His eyes looked his own height. He moved with the grace of an athlete. His skin was tanned by a wholesome outdoor life, and his eyes were clear and wide open. Physically he was a prince among men. We used to notice, as we marched along the road and passed other officers, that they always looked pleased to see him. They greeted him with a cordiality which was reserved for him. Even the general seemed to have singled him out, and cast an eye of special approval upon him. Somehow, gentle though he was, he was never familiar. He had a kind of innate nobility which marked him out as above us. He was not democratic. He was rather the justification for aristocracy. We all knew instinctively that he was our superior – a man of finer temper than ourselves, a "toff" in his own right. I suppose that that was why he could be so humble without loss of dignity. For he

was humble too, if that is the right word, and I think
it is. No trouble of ours was too small for him to
attend to. When we started route marches, for instance,
and our feet were blistered and sore, as they often
were at first, you would have thought that they were
his own feet from the trouble he took. Of course after
the march there was always an inspection of feet. That
is the routine. But with him it was no mere routine.
He came into our rooms, and if any one had a sore
foot he would kneel down on the floor and look at it
as carefully as if he had been a doctor. Then he would
prescribe, and the remedies were ready at hand, being
borne by the sergeant. If a blister had to be lanced he
would very likely lance it himself there and then, so
as to make sure that it was done with a clean needle
and that no dirt was allowed to get in. There was no
affectation about this, no striving after effect. It was
simply that he felt that our feet were pretty important,
and that he knew that we were pretty careless. So he
thought it best at the start to see to the matter himself.
Nevertheless, there was in our eyes something almost
religious about this care for our feet. It seemed to have
a touch of the Christ about it, and we loved and
honoured him the more.

> Donald Hankey, 'The Beloved Captain', *A
> Student in Arms* (1916), pp.64–6.

Hankey maintained that the common soldier, too, found his
true self through Army discipline.

> Instead of freedom, he found discipline. His uprisings
> and his outgoings, and all the smallest details of his
> being, even to the length of his hair and the cleanliness
> of his toes, were ordered by Powers against whom
> there was no appeal. They held all the trump cards.
> He could not even "chuck the job" in the old lordly
> way, without becoming a criminal, and having all the
> resources of the police enlisted to bring him back.
>   Yet the despotism, though complete, was not brutal.

Even the sergeant-major was genially abusive, while the subaltern was almost paternal. But these were only signs of the plenitude of their power. They could afford to be jovial! Indeed, he soon noticed that urbanity of manner was apt to increase in a direct ratio to an individual's rank. It was the corporal, the least of all his masters, whose manner was least conciliatory. Submission was obviously the only course; and by degrees he learnt to do more than submit. He learnt the pride of submission. He came to believe in the discipline. He gained self-respect from his subordination to it, and when he went home on furlough, wearing the uniform of it, he boasted of it, to the evident envy of his civilian chums. He was learning one of the great truths of life, a truth that so many fail to learn – that it is not in isolation but as a member of a body that a man finds his fullest self-expression: that it is not in self-assertion but in self-subordination, not as an individual but as one of many brethren, sons of one Father, that a man finds the complete satisfaction of his instincts, and the highest form of liberty.

> Donald Hankey, 'The Making of a Man', ibid.,
> pp.276–8.

Hankey's essays were published in book form in April 1916 and reprinted fourteen times in little more than a year. An unsympathetic observer might have remarked that they reinforced a class system which gave no scope to ordinary people for independent thought or initiative, leaving leadership to a trained élite. This would no doubt have been the opinion of the celebrated Australian journalist, C. E. W. Bean, whose Gallipoli diary gives a very different picture of the British Tommy in 1915.

Our men have a tremendous admiration for the little Gurkhas – they say they don't mind getting up against N.Z.s or Gurkhas – but they (and the N.Z. men too) do not trust the Tommy – they all except the regular army, but they have not the slightest confidence in

K[itchener]'s army – nor have our officers – nor have I. The truth is that after 100 years of breeding in slums, the British race is not the same, and can't be expected to be the same, as in the days of Waterloo. It is breeding one fine class at the expense of all the rest. The only hope is that those puny narrow-chested little men may, if they come out to Australia or N.Z. or Canada, within 2 generations breed men again. England herself, unless she does something heroic, cannot hope to. . . .

Well, the problem of Gallipoli reduces itself to – why can't the British fight? Take one of these slum kids and turn him into a different man by 9 or 10 years hard training, or even less – and put in a set of N.C.O.'s over him who have will enough to make the stickers of the army – the percentage who go into action with their minds made up to stick, and who really make up the minds of the other 90% who are simply going in to do what somebody else does; give him that training and those N.C.O.'s and he can fight like the 29th Division did. But in a year's training he can't be turned into a soldier because to tell the truth he's a very poor feeble specimen of a man – and it seems to be the British social formula to make sure that he sticks there. In a nation with only one class, it's in nobody's interest to keep anyone else in "his place" – and his place is, from his birth, the best place he can get and keep. To my mind this war, as far as I have seen it, is just Britain's tomahawks coming home to roost. . . They have neither the nerve, the physique, nor the spirit and self-control to fit them for soldiers. . . .

C. E. W. Bean, *Gallipoli Correspondent* (1983),
pp.153–5.

The Home Front

As was perhaps inevitable, heroes were more easily found on the far side of the Channel than at home. The intense national unity of August 1914 could never have lasted long. A gap began to widen between civilians and people on active service overseas. The older generation, despite – or because of – its best efforts to encourage the war effort, attracted growing resentment. At the end of April 1915, when the nation was mourning Brooke with rather too much rhetoric, a young subaltern wrote to *The Cambridge Magazine.*

> To many of us, the greatest trial that this war has brought is that it has released the old men from all restraining influences and has let them loose upon the world. The city Editors, the retired Majors, the Amazons, and last, but I fear not least, the Venerable Archdeacons, have never been so free from contradiction. Just when the younger generation was beginning to take its share in the affairs of the world, and was hoping to counteract the Victorian influences of the older generation, this war has come to silence us, – permanently or temporarily as the case may be. Meanwhile the old men are having field days on their own. In our name (and for OUR SAKES, as they pathetically imagine), they are doing their very utmost, it would seem, to perpetuate, by their appeals to hate, intolerance, and revenge, those very follies which have produced the present conflagration.
>
> Archibald Don, letter in *The Cambridge Magazine*, 1 May 1915 (reprinted 1 December 1917).

'Old men' had been unpopular before the war and were to be reviled after it; during it they were to be the butt of satirical verse by Sassoon (many of whose poems first appeared in *The Cambridge Magazine*), Owen, Osbert Sitwell and other soldier poets.

Divisions also grew within the Home Front. Politicians

competed for power, rival groups blamed each other for things that went wrong, and ideals faded. Wells, who, on the whole, had admired the popular response in 1914, was not alone in suffering disillusion. His changing feelings are recorded in his quasi-autobiographical 'novel', *Mr Britling Sees It Through*. Britling is a representative Briton, as his name suggests, but he is also very like his author, being a well-known journalist. When the book came out in September 1916, in the wake of the Somme, it became another bestseller; there were thirteen reprints before the year was out. It remains a valuable record of 1914–15 opinion. In the early spring of 1915 Britling's spirits fail as he considers the slaughter and confusion at the front and, even more dismaying, 'the collapse of the British mind from its first fine phase of braced-up effort into a state of bickering futility'.

Too long had British life been corrupted by the fictions of loyalty to an uninspiring and alien Court, of national piety in an official Church, of freedom in a politician-rigged State, of justice in an economic system where the advertiser, the sweater and usurer had a hundred advantages over the producer and artisan, to maintain itself now steadily at any high pitch of heroic endeavour. It had bought its comfort with the demoralisation of its servants. It had no completely honest organs; its spirit was clogged by its accumulated insincerities. Brought at last face to face with a bitter hostility and a powerful and unscrupulous enemy, an enemy socialistic, scientific and efficient to an unexampled degree, it seemed indeed to be inspired for a time by an unwonted energy and unanimity. Youth and the common people shone. The sons of every class went out to fight and die, full of a splendid dream of this war. Easy-going vanished from the foreground of the picture. But only to creep back again as the first inspiration passed. Presently the older men, the seasoned politicians, the owners and hucksters, the charming women and the habitual consumers, began to recover from this blaze of moral exaltation. Old habits of mind and procedure reasserted themselves. The war which had begun so dramatically missed its climax; there was neither heroic swift defeat nor heroic swift victory. There was indecision; the most trying test of all for an undisciplined people. There were great spaces of uneventful fatigue. Before the Battle of the Yser had fully developed the dramatic quality had gone out of the war. It had ceased to be either a tragedy or a triumph; for both sides it became a monstrous strain and wasting. It had become a wearisome thrusting against a pressure of evils. . . .

Under that strain the dignity of England broke, and revealed a malignity less focussed and intense than the German, but perhaps even more distressing. No paternal government had organised the British spirit for patriotic ends; it became now peevish and impatient, like some ill-trained man who is sick, it directed itself no longer against the enemy alone but fitfully against imagined traitors and shirkers; it wasted its energies in a deepening and spreading net of internal squabbles and accusations. Now it was the wily indolence of the Prime Minister, now it was the German culture of the Lord Chancellor, now the imaginative enterprise of the First Lord of the Admiralty that focussed a vindictive campaign. There began a hunt for spies and of suspects of German origin in every quarter except the highest; a denunciation now of "traitors," now of people with imaginations, now of scientific men, now of the personal friend of the Commander-in-Chief, now of this group and then of that group. . . . Every day Mr. Britling read his three or four newspapers with a deepening disappointment.

H. G. Wells, *Mr Britling Sees It Through* (1916), pp.288–9.

Not all the wartime quarrels at home were futile; some had profound effects on post-war society. In July 1915, for example, the South Wales miners struck for higher pay. Lloyd George, the new Minister for Munitions, was starting a huge programme of increased industrial production and could not risk a long dispute.

The Miners' Response

'We must keep on striking, striking, striking.' – First speech by the Minister of Munitions.

We do: the present desperate stage
Of fighting brings us luck;
And in the higher war we wage
(For higher wage) *We Struck.*

D. S. MacColl (dated 1915), *Bull and Other War Verses* (1919).

Whatever the ethics of the miners' action, it demonstrated the strength of the trade unions. One of the many side-effects of the war was a sudden increase in working-class wealth and power; there were jobs in plenty, as Government money poured into industry. By the 1920s the Labour Party, which had been created by the unions before the war as their political arm, had replaced the Liberals as one of the two main contenders for government, and the old world had indeed 'passed away', although not quite as Kipling and others had foretold.

Looking Beyond the War

Intellectuals of differing political beliefs shared the hope that the post-war world would achieve national and international democracy.

It will be necessary soon to consider the relations of democracy to the war. The war is a war of nationalities, but it was not made by peoples. Its begetter was a comparatively small band of unscrupulous, blind, and conceited persons, who were clever and persistent enough to demoralize a whole people. In so far as they permitted themselves to be demoralized the people were to blame, but the chief blame lies on the small band. Europe is laid waste, hundreds of thousands of men murdered, and practically every human being in the occidental hemisphere made to suffer, not for the amelioration of a race, but in order to satisfy the idiotic ambitions ˹ ᴀ handful. Let not this fact be forgotten. Democracy will not forget it. And foreign policy in the future will not be left in the hands of any autocracy, by whatever specious name the autocracy may call itself. Ruling classes have always said that masses were incapable of understanding foreign policy. The masses understand it now. They understand that in spite of very earnest efforts in various Cabinets, the ruling classes have failed to avert the most terrible disaster in history. The masses will say to themselves, 'At any rate we couldn't have done worse than that.' The masses know that if the war decision had been openly submitted to a representative German chamber, instead of being taken in conceal-ment and amid disgusting chicane, no war would have occurred. It is absolutely certain that the triumph of democracy, and nothing else, will end war as an institution. War will be ended when the Foreign Offices are subjected to popular control. That popular control is coming.

Arnold Bennett, *The Daily News*, 15 October 1914.

It might not be enough, however, to rely on the people for peace. Goldsworthy Lowes Dickinson, the Cambridge humanist and historian, pointed out that ordinary people tended to think in narrowly nationalist terms; they needed to be taught the value of international co-operation and law.

What I am urging is that the possibility of war depends at bottom on the existence in individual men and women of the habit of conceiving and feeling their State as independent of legal, moral, and cultural obligations to other States; of resenting, therefore, all attempts to develop such obligations; and thus regarding it as natural, inevitable, and right that disputes between States should be settled by war.

Now, this attitude of ordinary men and women is
the greatest obstacle to peace. For every attempt to
guarantee peace implies a willingness on the part of
the nations to submit their national causes, first, to
the rules of a common and recognized morality and
law; secondly, to formal institutions for the application
and enforcement of those rules. This is true of every
conceivable scheme, from the loosest and freest league
to a complete system of international government.
There need be, and should be, nothing in any such
schemes incompatible with the true interests of nationality, nor with the genuine and desirable autonomy of
States. Internationalism does not attack the feeling "We
belong to ourselves." It attacks only its perversion,
"We do not belong to you." And this point goes very
deep. The future of civilization after this war will
depend upon the decision of the question whether it
is their independence or their inter-dependence that
the nations will stress. The former course leads to a
series of wars, the latter to peace. The issue is even
now joined. In the passion of war there are those who
urge, and apparently with conviction, that national
excellence and security lie in the completest possible
isolation; in excluding foreigners and foreign trade; in
exaggerating and perpetuating national differences and
national antagonisms; in fostering, as the chief good,
national egotism. That way lies the ruin of Western
civilization. For everything that makes for civilization
is international. The nations of the West are far more
alike than they are unlike, and their points of likeness
are much more important than their points of unlike-
ness. Not only materially but spiritually every nation
is poorer by breach of contact with any other. The
sole point in which the nations are independent is that
of government. That they should retain their political
autonomy is desirable, so long as they wish to retain
it. And to attempt to bring one of them by force under
the government of another is a crime, as well as a folly.
But for the growing life of nations, what they need is
contacts. Nor is it possible to avoid them. The ideal

of independence, spiritual, moral, intellectual, or economic, is as impracticable as it is undesirable. But even
a partial movement in that direction may do much
harm. For it must increase misunderstandings and
points of friction, and so lead to further wars. The
cause of peace is the cause of internationalism; the
cause of internationalism is the cause of civilization;
and the enemy of all these is "corporate egotism."

> G. K. Dickinson, 'The Basis of Permanent Peace',
> in *Towards a Lasting Settlement*, ed. C. R.
> Buxton (1915), pp.25–7.

Dickinson was a leading voice in the movement for a 'League
of Nations', a term he is said to have invented. Another of
the Great War's side-effects was the establishment in the
1920s of the League and of affiliated organisations such as the
Permanent Court of International Justice at The Hague. Many
international bodies of our own time, including the United
Nations, the International Court of Justice, and the EEC,
could be said to have their roots in the Great War and in the
earnest civilian debates which accompanied it.

Wartime speculation on the origins, nature, purpose and
results of the conflict was wide-ranging and prolific, most of
it coming from civilians and little of it proving to be of any
lasting value. Emotions were high, but very few people really
knew what was happening, either in politics or on the
battlefields. Opinions ranged from those of E. D. Morel,
who blamed Britain for the war, to those of Cecil Chesterton,
who, like his more famous brother, saw Europe as Catholic
'Christendom' menaced now as in Roman and medieval times
by pagan barbarians from the East. Chesterton maintained
that Prussia was nothing less than the legendary Vampire.
Edward Carpenter, the prophet of Socialism and sexual
liberation, wondered aloud whether war was not an expression
of the sex-drive. There was much else; probably no period
in previous history had produced such an immense amount
of printed matter.

The End of 1915

Whatever theory might be put forward to explain what was happening, there was no disguising the fact that things were not going well. 1914 had at least ended with the German advance halted in the West and German long-distance sea power finished, but 1915 brought no such comforts. Attempts to circumvent the stalemate in Europe were not successful. The decaying Turkish Empire had joined the Central Powers in October 1914, giving Britain and France the chance to make territorial gains in what is now called the Middle East, but a British–Indian force which had begun a campaign in Mesopotamia was trapped at Kut in November 1915 and suffered a ghastly siege. A bold expedition to the Dardanelles in April 1915 failed to get beyond the Gallipoli beaches and was called off at the end of the year. Another Mediterranean landing in October established an Allied force at Salonika but made no further progress. Serbia had been destroyed, and Bulgaria had joined the wrong side. On Germany's Eastern Front, Russian casualties were appalling. The Western Front nowhere moved more than three miles during the year. The generals continued to think, all the same, that if victory could be achieved anywhere it would be in France and Flanders. Once the munitions industry had reached full production and Kitchener's New Armies had completed their training, a 'Big Push' might drive the enemy backwards by sheer force of artillery and numbers. The insatiable demand for 'More men and still more men' revived the pre-war pressure for conscription, on the grounds that the best men had enlisted while 'shirkers' had stayed at home. With fewer husbands and more money about, family ties came under strain and there was concern for public morals. Despite traditional dislike of state power, government controls over the nation's life were becoming all-pervasive, yet Asquith's administration, now a coalition of Liberals and Conservatives, was losing public confidence. The country's determination did not falter, but the goodwill of 1914 did not survive 1915.

The year was a testing time for writers. Some fell into despair, some found new faith. D. H. Lawrence, for example, who had completed his novel *The Rainbow* on a note of

INJURED INNOCENCE.

THE GERMAN OGRE. "HEAVEN KNOWS THAT I HAD TO DO THIS IN SELF-DEFENCE;
IT WAS FORCED UPON ME." (*Aside*) "FEE, FI, FO, FUM!"

[According to the Imperial Chancellor's latest utterance Germany is the deeply-wronged victim of British militarism.]

1. *Injured Innocence* by Bernard Partridge, *Punch* (31 May 1916), page 361. The German Ogre stands on the torn 'scrap of paper', the treaty which had guaranteed Belgian neutrality. Behind him is Bernhardi's slogan, 'Weltmacht oder Niedergang' ('World-power or downfall'). Photograph © Bodleian Library, from *N. 2706 d 10*.

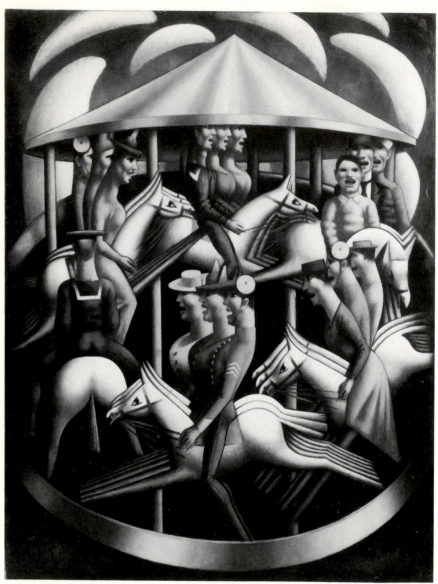

2. *The Merry-Go-Round* by Mark Gertler (1916). ' . . . in this combination of blaze, and violent and mechanised rotation and complete involution, utterly mindless intensity of sensational extremity, you have made a real and ultimate revelation' (D. H. Lawrence to Gertler, 9 October 1916). Photograph © Tate Gallery.

3. *The Signing of the Peace in the Hall of Mirrors, 28 June 1919* by William Orpen. In front of the leaders of the victorious countries, German representatives sign the Treaty of Versailles. The overwhelming architecture and crooked mirrors make a mocking background. One of the reflected silhouettes is Orpen himself, official British artist at the conference. Photograph © The Trustees of the Imperial War Museum.

4. *The Menin Road 1918* by Adrian Hill. British troops pass through the site of the old town gate in the walls of Ypres. Plates 4 and 5 were published together as No 1 in a series 'Ten Years After 1918–1928' in *Answers Magazine* (20 October 1928). Photograph © Bodleian Library, from *John Johnson Collection: Great War. Box 24.*

5. *The Menin Gate 1928* by Adrian Hill. The new gate, completed in 1927, is a memorial to the armies of the British Empire who held the Ypres Salient; it bears the names of 54 889 soldiers who have no known graves. Photograph © Bodleian Library, from *John Johnson Collection: Great War. Box 24.*

optimism in March 1915, came to feel by the autumn that the British people were without honour or values.

> Those days, that autumn . . . people carried about crysanthemums, yellow and brown crysanthemums: and the smell of burning leaves: and the wounded, bright blue soldiers with their red cotton neckties, sitting together like macaws on the seats, pale and different from other people. And the star Jupiter very bright at nights over the cup hollow of the Vale, on Hampstead Heath. And the war news coming, the war horror drifting in, drifting in, prices rising, excitement growing, people going mad about the Zeppelin raids. And always the one song:

> Keep the home fires burning,
> Though your hearts are yearning.

> It was in 1915 the old world ended. In the winter 1915–1916 the spirit of the old London collapsed; the city, in some way, perished, perished from being a heart of the world, and became a vortex of broken passions, lusts, hopes, fears, and horrors. The integrity of London collapsed, and the genuine debasement began, the unspeakable baseness of the press and the public voice, the reign of that bloated ignominy, *John Bull*.

> No man who has really consciously lived through this can believe again absolutely in democracy. No man who has heard reiterated in thousands of tones from all the common people during the crucial years of the war: 'I believe in *John Bull*. Give me *John Bull*,' can ever believe that in any crisis a people can govern itself, or is ever fit to govern itself. During the crucial years of the war, the people chose, and chose Bottomleyism. Bottom enough.

> The well-bred, really cultured classes were on the whole passive resisters. They shirked their duty. It is the business of people who really know better to fight tooth and nail to keep up a standard, to hold control

of authority. *Laisser-aller* is as guilty as the actual, stinking mongrelism it gives place to.

D. H. Lawrence, 'The Nightmare', *Kangaroo*
(1923), chapter 10.

This contempt for democracy led Lawrence into some strange thoughts – at times he argued for a British Kaiser, even for mass exterminations – but out of his wretchedness and fury were to come *Women in Love* and many poems.

A much more positive view of current events came from Wells, whose low spirits earlier in the year were replaced in the autumn by what he took to be a religious awakening, an experience he passed on to Mr Britling. (In the novel, Britling's son, Hugh, and a young German friend, Heinrich, have been killed.)

He sat back in his chair wearily, with his chin sunk upon his chest. For a time he did not think, and then, he read again the sentence in front of his eyes.

'These boys, these hopes, this war has killed.'

The words hung for a time in his mind.

'No!' said Mr. Britling stoutly. 'They live!'

And suddenly it was borne in upon his mind that he was not alone. There were thousands and tens of thousands of men and women like himself, desiring with all their hearts to say, as he desired to say, the reconciling word. It was not only his hand that thrust against the obstacles. . . . Frenchmen and Russians sat in the same stillness, facing the same perplexities; there were Germans seeking a way through to him. Even as he sat and wrote. And for the first time clearly he felt a Presence of which he had thought very many times in the last few weeks, a Presence so close to him that it was behind his eyes and in his brain and hands. It was no trick of his vision; it was a feeling of immediate reality. And it was Hugh, Hugh that he had thought was dead, it was young Heinrich living also, it was himself, it was those others that sought, it was all these and it was more, it was the Master, the Captain of Mankind, it was God, there present with him, and he knew that it was God. It was as if he had been groping all this time in the darkness, thinking himself alone amidst rocks and pitfalls and pitiless things, and suddenly a hand, a firm strong hand, had touched his own. And a voice within him bade him be of good courage. There was no magic trickery in that moment; he was still weak and weary, a discouraged rhetorician, a good intention ill-equipped; but he was no longer lonely and wretched, no longer in the same world with despair. God was beside him and within him and about him. . . . It was the crucial moment of Mr. Britling's life. It was a thing as light as the passing of a cloud on an April morning; it was a thing as great as the first day of creation [. . . .]

There was no need to despair because he himself was one of the feeble folk. God was with him indeed, and he was with God. The King was coming to his own. Amidst the darknesses and confusions, the nightmare cruelties and the hideous stupidities of the great war, God, the Captain of the World Republic, fought his way to empire. So long as one did one's best and utmost in a cause so mighty, did it matter though the thing one did was little and poor?

'I have thought too much of myself,' said Mr. Britling, 'and of what I would do by myself. I have forgotten *that which was with me*. . . .'

H. G. Wells, *Mr Britling Sees It Through* (1916), pp.438–9.

This creed of a war that would not only end war but also bring God's kingdom on earth owed much less to Christianity than to Wells's frequent advocacy of a World State under the control of enlightened men, for he was an ardent internationalist. He later said that his new religious faith had been a wartime aberration. Perhaps Mr Britling's moment of vision was typical of the religious feelings which war arouses in people who are not normally of a spiritual disposition. Britling is certainly typical, at any rate, at the end of the year (and of the book) when he resolves to see the war through; most of his fellow Britons would have agreed with that, even after the disappointments of 1915.

4 The Year of the Somme: 1916

Realism, Yet Romance Lingers

1916 saw the end of amateurishness and the volunteer spirit. Conscription was introduced at the beginning of the year, for the first time in the nation's history; it was generally accepted as fair, to the Government's relief. Agreement was reached with France for the Big Push in the summer and meticulous planning got under way. The Gallipoli campaign was closed when the last troops withdrew in January, a moment described by John Masefield.

> In the haze of the full moon the men filed off from the trenches down to the beaches, and passed away from Gallipoli, from the unhelped attempt which they had given their bodies and their blood to make. They had lost no honour. They were not to blame, that they were creeping off in the dark, like thieves in the night. Had others (not of their profession), many hundreds of miles away, but been as they, as generous, as wise, as foreseeing, as full of sacrifice, those thinned companies with the looks of pain in their faces, and the mud of the hills thick upon their bodies, would have given thanks in Santa Sophia three months before. They had failed to take Gallipoli, and the mine-fields still barred the Hellespont, but they had fought a battle such as has never been seen upon this earth. What they had done will become a glory for ever, wherever the deeds of heroic unhelped men are honoured and pitied and understood. They went up at the call of duty, with a bright banner of a battle-cry, against an impregnable fort. Without guns, without munitions, without help, and without drink, they climbed the scarp, and held it by their own glorious manhood, quickened by a word from their chief. Now they were giving back

89

the scarp, and going out into new adventures, wherever the war might turn.

Those going down to the beaches wondered in a kind of awe whether the Turks would discover them and attack. The minutes passed, and boat after boat left the shore, but no attack came. The arranged rifles fired mechanically in the outer trenches at long intervals, and the crackle of the Turk reply followed. At Anzac, a rearguard of honour had been formed. The last two hundred men to leave Anzac were survivors of those who had landed in the first charge, so glorious and so full of hope, on the 25th of April. They had fought through the whole campaign from the very beginning; they had seen it all. It was only just that they should be the last to leave. As they, too, moved down, one of their number saw a solitary Turk, black against the sky. . . .

John Masefield, *Gallipoli* (1916), pp.176–7.

Masefield's book, a romantic-heroic account written for the propaganda authorities at his own request, eased the humiliation of defeat and proved very popular. He had visited the beaches in 1915 and then gone on a lecture tour in America, where American and German mockery of the campaign prompted him to write in its defence. He exonerated the soldiers involved, putting the blame on the organisers at home. Similar criticism was levelled at the horrors and incompetence of the Mesopotamia disaster; Kipling's often-anthologised poem 'Mesopotamia' is a savage attack on the mismanagement which led to the fall of Kut in April, but he, like Masefield, remained a firm supporter of the war itself. The emphasis in 1916 was to be on such matters as efficiency, careful preparation and adequate supplies; there were to be no more brave adventures.

The romance of war died hard, remaining a possibility in fiction and occasionally even in fact on the edges of the fighting. John Buchan's *Greenmantle* (1916) describes the dramatic role played by a British agent at the Russian capture of Erzerum in February 1916, a story based on the adventures of an actual agent, Aubrey Herbert. Buchan's three Richard Hannay novels were popular among soldiers, who found them just realistic enough to be convincing but enthrallingly fast-moving, compared to the boredom of the Western Front. Buchan wrote fiction tinged with fact, but T. E. Lawrence's extraordinary exploits in Arabia, later described in his *Seven Pillars of Wisdom* (1935), were fact tinged with fiction. Lawrence's legendary quality is rooted in his own writing as well as in his actions, making him an endlessly fascinating subject for films, plays, biographies and journalism.

The Arabs passed before us into a little sunken place, which rose to a low crest; and we knew that the hill beyond went down in a facile slope to the main valley of Aba el Lissan, somewhat below the spring. All our four hundred camel men were here tightly collected, just out of sight of the enemy. We rode to their head, and asked the Shimt what it was and where the horsemen had gone.

He pointed over the ridge to the next valley above us, and said, 'With Auda there': and as he spoke yells and shots poured up in a sudden torrent from beyond the crest. We kicked our camels furiously to the edge, to see our fifty horsemen coming down the last slope into the main valley like a run-away, at full gallop, shooting from the saddle. As we watched, two or three went down, but the rest thundered forward at marvellous speed, and the Turkish infantry, huddled together under the cliff ready to cut their desperate way out towards Maan, in the first dusk began to sway in and out, and finally broke before the rush, adding their flight to Auda's charge.

Nasir screamed at me, 'Come on', with his bloody mouth; and we plunged our camels madly over the hill, and down towards the head of the fleeing enemy. The slope was not too steep for a camel-gallop, but steep enough to make their pace terrific, and their course uncontrollable: yet the Arabs were able to extend to right and left and to shoot into the Turkish brown. The Turks had been too bound up in the terror of Auda's furious charge against their rear to notice us as we came over the eastward slope: so we also took them by surprise and in the flank; and a charge of ridden camels going nearly thirty miles an hour was irresistible.

My camel, the Sherari racer, Naama, stretched herself out, and hurled downhill with such might that we soon out-distanced the others. The Turks fired a few shots, but mostly only shrieked and turned to run: the bullets they did send at us were not very harmful, for it took much to bring a charging camel down in a dead heap.

I had got among the first of them, and was shooting, with a pistol of course, for only an expert could use a rifle from such plunging beasts; when suddenly my camel tripped and went down emptily upon her face, as though pole-axed. I was torn completely from the saddle, sailed grandly through the air for a great distance, and landed with a crash which seemed to drive all the power and feeling out of me. I lay there, passively waiting for the Turks to kill me, continuing to hum over the verses of a half-forgotten poem, whose rhythm something, perhaps the prolonged stride of the camel, had brought back to my memory as we leaped down the hill-side:

> For Lord I was free of all Thy flowers, but I chose
> the world's sad roses,
> And that is why my feet are torn and mine eyes are
> blind with sweat.

While another part of my mind thought what a squashed thing I should look when all that cataract of men and camels had poured over.

After a long time I finished my poem, and no Turks came, and no camel trod on me: a curtain seemed taken from my ears: there was a great noise in front. I sat up and saw the battle over, and our men driving together and cutting down the last remnants of the enemy. My camel's body had lain behind me like a rock and divided the charge into two streams: and in

the back of its skull was the heavy bullet of the fifth
shot I fired.

T. E. Lawrence, *Seven Pillars of Wisdom* (1935),
pp.235–6.

It seems incongruous that Lawrence began his leadership of
the Arab Revolt, with its adventures, camel charges, swift
victories and unorthodox warfare, in 1916, the year of Verdun
and the Somme.

There was another revolt in 1916 that evoked romantic
feelings, the Easter Rising in Dublin. Home Rule for Ireland
had been under serious consideration just before the war, but
it had been thwarted by the threat of armed resistance in the
North. Large numbers of Irishmen, from the South as well as
the North, had then joined in the fight against Germany, so
that sympathy for the rebels was limited; but the shelling of
Dublin and the executions of sixteen ringleaders provoked
strong feelings. For Yeats, a 'terrible beauty' was born ('Easter
1916'); the vision of a free Ireland would seem more important
than the defeat of Germany, now that the Irish had new
martyrs to add to their long list.

O but we talked at large before
The sixteen men were shot,
But who can talk of give and take,
What should be and what not
While those dead men are loitering there
To stir the boiling pot?

You say that we should still the land
Till Germany's overcome;
But who is there to argue that
Now Pearse is deaf and dumb?
And is their logic to outweigh
MacDonagh's bony thumb?

How could you dream they'd listen
That have an ear alone
For those new comrades they have found,

Lord Edward and Wolfe Tone,
Or meddle with our give and take
That converse bone to bone?

W. B. Yeats, 'Sixteen Dead Men', *Michael
Robartes and the Dancer* (1920).

For the British, on the other hand, the Irish rebellion was an
exasperating diversion from the main business in hand. The
Germans had launched a colossal offensive in February against
the French stronghold of Verdun, making an Allied response
elsewhere in the line more urgent than ever.

Poets in Wartime

Secrecy about the coming assault was scarcely possible, since
the whole nation seemed to be caught up in preparations for
it. The war effort was becoming a vast machine. Perhaps the
fighting would be brought to an end at last, but the bigger
the war grew the more insane it seemed that a nation's wealth,
skill, and youth should be devoted to destroying those of
another. In February Sassoon wrote his first sceptical war
poem, 'In the Pink' ('And still the war goes on – *he*
don't know why'), and Edward Thomas wrote 'February
Afternoon'.

Men heard this roar of parleying starlings, saw,
A thousand years ago even as now,
Black rooks with white gulls following the plough
So that the first are last until a caw
Commands that last are first again, – a law
Which was of old when one, like me, dreamed how
A thousand years might dust lie on his brow
Yet thus would birds do between hedge and shaw.

Time swims before me, making as a day
A thousand years, while the broad ploughland oak
Roars mill-like and men strike and bear the stroke

Of war as ever, audacious or resigned,
And God still sits aloft in the array
That we have wrought him, stone-deaf and stone-
blind.

Edward Thomas, 'February Afternoon', *Last
Poems* (1918).

The muted resignation of Thomas's tone expresses the temper
of the mid-war years as well as his personal acceptance of an
obligation to enlist and fight. No officer in training in early
1916 could be in much doubt about his own likely future.

Another poet who wrote about this period of the war was
David Jones, whose *In Parenthesis* is in a style quite unlike
Thomas's. Jones remembered how life in the trenches alter-
nated between bouts of heavy shelling and long stretches of
inaction, including nights of sentry-duty when rats' feet made
the only sound.

> You can hear the silence of it:
> you can hear the rat of no-man's-land
> rut-out intricacies,
> weasel-out his patient workings,
> scrut, scrut, sscrut,
> harrow out-earthly, trowel his cunning paw;
> redeem the time of our uncharity, to sap his own
>   amphibious paradise.
> You can hear his carrying-parties rustle our corrup-
> tions through the night-weeds – contest the choicest
> morsels in his tiny conduits, bead-eyed feast on us;
> by a rule of his nature, at night-feast on the broken of
> us.
> Those broad-pinioned;
> blue-burnished, or brinded-back;
> whose proud eyes watched
>   the broken emblems
> droop and drag dust,
> suffer with us this metamorphosis.
> These too have shed their fine feathers; these too
> have slimed their dark-bright coats; these too have
> condescended to dig in.

    The white-tailed eagle at the battle ebb,
               where the sea wars against the river
    the speckled kite of Maldon
    and the crow
    have naturally selected to be un-winged;
    to go on the belly, to
    sap sap sap
    with festered spines, arched under the moon; furrit
      with
    whiskered snouts the secret parts of us.
    When it's all quiet you can hear them:
    scrut scrut scrut
    when it's as quiet as this is.
    It's so very still.
    Your body fits the crevice of the bay in the most
    comfortable fashion imaginable.
    It's cushy enough.

    The relief elbows him on the fire-step: All quiet
    china? – bugger all to report? – kipping mate? – christ,
    mate – you'll 'ave 'em all over.

          David Jones, *In Parenthesis* (1937), Part III.

Jones combines myth and experience, the one illustrating the other, as in his image of the wartime rat as a featherless, inglorious version of the birds of prey described in an Anglo-Saxon poem about the battle of Maldon. The status of *In Parenthesis* has been a matter for debate; some critics have argued that its mythical dimension is a falsification of experience, while others have made strong claims for it as one of the great poems of the century. It is certainly unlike the poetry written during the war, being long, retrospective, meditative, and composed in a learned, Modernist style not fully available to any British poet in 1914–18.

    Jones's rat may be compared with Isaac Rosenberg's in a famous poem written in France in June 1916.

    The darkness crumbles away.
    It is the same old druid Time as ever,
    Only a live thing leaps my hand,
    A queer sardonic rat,

As I pull the parapet's poppy
To stick behind my ear.
Droll rat, they would shoot you if they knew
Your cosmopolitan sympathies.
Now you have touched this English hand
You will do the same to a German
Soon, no doubt, if it be your pleasure
To cross the sleeping green between.
It seems you inwardly grin as you pass
Strong eyes, fine limbs, haughty athletes
Less chanced than you for life,
Bonds to the whims of murder,
Sprawled in the bowels of the earth,
The torn fields of France.
What do you see in our eyes
At the shrieking iron and flame
Hurled through still heavens?
What quaver – what heart aghast?
Poppies whose roots are in man's veins
Drop, and are ever dropping;
But mine in my ear is safe –
Just a little white with the dust.

> Isaac Rosenberg, 'Break of Day in the Trenches',
> *Poetry* (Chicago: December 1916).

The rat here is a 'sardonic' creature, more aware of contemporary politics than of the legendary past. It is more confident of its survival than the poet can be of his own, the transience of which is symbolised by the poppy, a flower which shrivels within moments of being picked. Men have made themselves inferior to rats. As in Thomas's sonnet (the two poems have more in common than may at first appear), the ancient movements and forces of nature continue in war as in peace; time, the bringer of change, is itself unchanging, but human life lasts no longer than the flower of the field. In jauntily putting the poppy behind his ear, Rosenberg makes a brave gesture, like some Elizabethan adventurer facing death.

There were many brave gestures in the trenches, as men strengthened the line, waited for the offensive and endured endless raids. Ivor Gurney, a Private in the Gloucesters, recorded in a June letter the 'Song that Signallers Sung and Stretcherbearers of C Company, when the great guns roared at them and the Germans thought to attack'.

> I want to go Home
> I want to go home
> the whizz bangs and shrapnel they whistle and roar.
> I don't want to go on the top any more.
> Take me over the sea
> where the allemans [Germans] can't catch me
> O my I don't want to die
> I want to go Home.

(The famous soldier songs of the war have not been fully chronicled, but it is inaccurate to suppose that they all express bitterness and belong to the later stages of the war; for example, 'Send out my mother, my sister, or my brother, / But for Gawd's sake don't send me' was popular at Aldershot in October 1914.) Gurney's letter expresses the same defiantly humorous mixture of longing to go home and refusing to give up or give in.

> We have . . . gone through a strafe which a machine-gunner who had been through Loos said was worse than Loos while it lasted – which was for 1¼ hours. And it left me exalted and exulting only longing for a nice blighty that would have taken me away from all this and left me free to play the G minor Prelude from the Second Book of Bach. O for a good piano! I am tired of this war, it bores me; but I would not willingly give up such a memory of such a time. Everything went wrong, and there was a tiny panic at first – but everybody, save the officers, were doing what they ought to do, and settled down later to the proper job, but if Fritz expected us as much as we expected them, he must have been in a funk. But they behaved very well our men, and one bay filled with signallers and stretcher bearers sang lustily awhile a song [see above] . . . very popular out here, but not at all military in

feeling. The machine guns are the most terrifying of sound, like an awful pack of hell hounds at ones back. I was out mending wires part of the time, but they were not so bad then. 10 high explosives were sailing over the signaller dugout and the bay where I was in front of it. A foot would have made a considerable difference to us I think. They burst about 30 yards behind. Their explosives are not nearly so terrible as ours. You can see dugouts and duckboards sailing in the air. . . . Theirs of course do damage enough, but nothing comparable. They began it, and were reduced to showing white lights, which we shot away, and sending up a white rocket. Floreat Gloucestriensis! It was a great time; full of fear of course, but not so bad as neurasthenia. I could have written letters through the whole of it. But O to be back out of it all! We had a gross casualties or more – some damned good men among them. Two chaps especially, whom I hoped to meet after the war. The writing in the latter part of this letter will be very bad – myself having come off the worse in a single handed combat with a bully-beef tin; but the bandage looks interesting.

Ivor Gurney, *War Letters* (1983), pp.74–5.

Gurney has always been known as a musician, but the publication of his war letters and many previously unknown war poems has drawn attention to him as a lively correspondent and outstanding poet. That 'single handed combat with a bully-beef tin' speaks volumes for his mood in June 1916 and for his admiration for his fellow soldiers, feelings which are recorded more seriously in his wartime poems.

Gurney's letters from the front gloss over the horrors. Most soldiers were similarly reticent, knowing from experience that the average civilian would either be distressed or fail to understand. For this and other reasons civilians often seemed to be unaware of horrors, an 'insensibility' (Owen's word) very different from the ironic cheerfulness of the troops. Occasionally soldiers would react by writing in angry detail to someone who would sympathise and perhaps help to spread the truth. T. S. Eliot read a letter of this kind and sent it to *The Nation*, identifying the author only as a subaltern who had joined up directly from public school at the age of eighteen.

> I have often heard it said that the curious thing about those who have been to the front is their complete indifference. . . . The impression one has from them is that [war] is, on the whole, a dreary and unpleasant business, with its anxious moments and its bright moments, but not nearly such a hell as one really knows it to be.
>
> In the case of the vast majority, however, this is an attitude, a screen – I speak of educated, thinking men – and it is not granted to many who have not shared the same experiences to see behind this screen. . . . [The] uninitiated [cannot] . . . realise or imagine even dimly the actual conditions of war. And a man who has been through it and seen and taken part in the unspeakable tragedies that are the ordinary routine, feels that he has something, possesses something, which others can never possess.
>
> It is morally impossible for him to talk seriously of these things to people who cannot even approach comprehension. It is hideously exasperating to hear people talking the glib commonplaces about the war and distributing cheap sympathy to its victims.
>
> Perhaps you are tempted to give them a picture of a leprous earth, scattered with the swollen and blackening corpses of hundreds of young men. The appalling stench of rotting carrion mingled with the sickening smell of exploded lyddite and ammonal. Mud like porridge, trenches like shallow and sloping cracks in the porridge – porridge that stinks in the sun. Swarms of flies and bluebottles clustering on pits of offal. Wounded men lying in the shell holes among the decaying corpses: helpless under the scorching sun and bitter nights, under repeated shelling. Men with bowels dropping out, lungs shot away, with blinded, smashed faces, or limbs blown into space. Men screaming and

gibbering. Wounded men hanging in agony on the barbed wire, until a friendly spout of liquid fire shrivels them up like a fly in a candle. But these are only words, and probably only convey a fraction of their meaning to their hearers. They shudder, and it is forgotten. . . .

Anon, quoted by T. S. Eliot in a letter to *The Nation*, 23 June 1917.

Few accounts like this were published during the war, even in a progressive journal such as *The Nation*. The silence covering trench experience was stronger than official censorship. As Eliot's correspondent said, no words could bridge the gap. But words could at least show that the gap existed and the information which trickled back has weighed ever since on the British imagination. It is sometimes said that no civilians knew about conditions at the front until the flood of 'war books' in the late twenties, but not everyone at home was in ignorance. Eliot, for one, was tormented by what he knew.

Despite the horrors, there appeared to be some grounds for hope. The Push was going to be so big that failure seemed impossible. The Germans were having no success at Verdun and the Austrian invasion of Italy seemed to be getting nowhere. The German Navy, having ventured out to sea at the end of May, met the British Grand Fleet off Jutland and retired after a fierce engagement. It was possible to consider Jutland a British victory; the Germans sank more ships than they lost, but failed to break the Allied blockade. In the East the Russians were at last beginning to drive the Austrians back. British newspapers were optimistic. The military authorities must have been less confident, knowing that their plans depended on troops who were still largely untried in battle; they organised the coming offensive with anxious care, like the thorough-minded Victorians they were.

The mood of many of the troops is perhaps reflected in Gurney's letter. Among the subalterns who would lead the attack, states of mind varied greatly. Sassoon was not the only one who had lost the Brooke-like fervour of 1914–15.

Some had lost all their convictions, including religious faith.

> One writes to me to ask me if I've read
> Of 'the Jutland battle', of 'the great advance
> Made by the Russians', chiding – 'History
> Is being made these days, these are the things
> That *are* worth while.'
>   These!
>   Not to one who's lain
> In Heaven before God's throne with eyes abased,
> Worshipping Him, in many forms of Good,
> That sate thereon; turning this patchwork world
> Wholly to glorify Him, point His plan
> Toward some supreme perfection, dimly visioned
> By loving faith: not these to him, when, stressed
> By some soul-dizzying woe beyond his trust
> He lifts his startled face, and finds the Throne
> Empty, and turns away, too drunk with Truth
> To mind his shame, or feel the loss of God.

>   Arthur Graeme West, 'The End of the Second
>   Year', *Diary of a Dead Officer* (1919).

It may be, though, that West's loss of Christian belief was less typical than W. N. Hodgson's better-known commitment, expressed in a poem published (but not necessarily written) at the end of June, a few days before its author's death.

> By all the glories of the day
>   And the cool evening's benison,
> By that last sunset touch that lay
>   Upon the hills when day was done,
> By beauty lavishly outpoured
>   And blessings carelessly received,
> By all the days that I have lived
>   Make me a soldier, Lord.

> By all of all man's hopes and fears,
>   And all the wonders poets sing,
> The laughter of unclouded years,
>   And every sad and lovely thing;

By the romantic ages stored
  With high endeavour that was his,
By all his mad catastrophes
  Make me a man, O Lord.

I, that on my familiar hill
  Saw with uncomprehending eyes
A hundred of Thy sunsets spill
  Their fresh and sanguine sacrifice,
Ere the sun swings his noonday sword
  Must say good-bye to all of this; –
By all delights that I shall miss,
  Help me to die, O Lord.

W. N. Hodgson, 'Before Action', *The New
Witness* (29 June 1916).

1 July

The British offensive on the Somme opened on 1 July, after
days of continuous bombardment. The depth and strength of
the German fortifications had not been fully understood. As
soon as the barrage moved forward to fall on the enemy
support trenches and allow the advance to begin, machine-
gunners emerged unscathed from their concrete dug-outs in
the German front line. In the southern sector the attack took
a substantial amount of ground, but in the north it ran into
difficulties; the protective barrage could not be recalled,
thanks to the careful rigidity of the battle plan, and men
were slaughtered in tens of thousands. That day is often
remembered as the worst in British history, but there have
been other ways of describing it. Arthur Conan Doyle was
more positive; commissioned by the War Office to chronicle
the Western campaign, he wrote while the war was still in
progress.

When the sun set upon that bloody day – probably
the most stirring of any single day in the whole record
of the world – the higher command of the Allies must

have looked upon the result with a strange mixture of feelings, in which dismay at the losses in the north and pride at the successes in the south contended for the mastery. The united losses of all the combatants, British, French, and Germans, must have been well over 100,000 between the rising and the setting of one summer sun. It is a rout which usually swells the casualties of a stricken army, but here there was no question of such a thing, and these huge losses were incurred in actual battle. As the attackers our own casualties were undoubtedly heavier than those of the enemy, and it is natural that as we turn from that list we ask ourselves the question whether our gains were worth it. Such a question might be an open one at Neuve Chapelle or at Loos, but here the answer must be a thousand times Yes. Together we had done the greatest day's work in the War up to that time – a day's work which led to many developments in the future, and eventually to a general German retreat over 70 miles of front. It was not a line of trenches which we broke, it was in truth the fortified frontier of Germany built up by a year and a half of unremitting labour. By breaking it at one point we had outflanked it from the Somme to the sea, and however slow the process might be of getting room for our forces to deploy, and pushing the Germans off our flank, it was certain that sooner or later that line must be rolled up from end to end. It was hoped, too, that under our gunfire no other frontier of similar strength could grow up in front of us. That was the great new departure which may be dated from July 1, and is an ample recompense for our losses. These young lives were gladly laid down as a price for final victory – and history may show that it was really on those Picardy slopes that final victory was in truth ensured.

A. Conan Doyle, *The British Campaign in France and Flanders 1916* (Spring 1918), pp. 100–1.

Doyle was too optimistic. His guess at the number of men

killed, missing and wounded conceals the enormous imbalance on that day between German losses (about 6000) and British (about 60 000). The German 'retreat over 70 miles of front' early in 1917 was not a retreat but a deliberate straightening of the line. There are modern historians, nevertheless, who share his – and Haig's – view that the Somme has to be understood as a first move in a larger strategy, a necessary step towards victory in 1918; they point out that commentators who regard the battles of 1916–17 as futile tend to overlook the fact that the war was concluded by military victory, not by chance or universal collapse. However, the strategy of General Haig and his colleagues has more often been condemned than defended. Some of its harshest critics included the politicians who had ultimate responsibility for it; among these was Lloyd George, who had been a leading 'Easterner', arguing that the war could not be won by attrition in the West. Strangly, Lloyd George worked with the 'Westerners' after the Somme, declaring that the fight had to be 'to a finish'; his commitment to victory enabled him to take Asquith's place as Prime Minister by the end of the year, but he made no attempt to dismiss Haig.

Haig himself repeatedly explained that an all-out continuous offensive on the Western Front was the only route to victory. He summed up his thinking about the Somme in a note of 1 August 1916.

(*a*) Pressure on Verdun relieved. Not less than six enemy Divns. besides heavy guns have been withdrawn.

(*b*) Successes achieved by Russia last month would certainly have been prevented had enemy been free to transfer troops from here to the Eastern Theatre.

(*c*) Proof given to world that Allies are capable of making and maintaining a vigorous offensive and of driving enemy's best troops from the strongest positions has shaken faith of Germans, of their friends, of doubting neutrals in the invincibility of Germany. Also impressed on the world, England's strength and determination, and the fighting power of the British race.

(*d*) We have inflicted very heavy losses on the enemy. In *one* month, 30 of his Divns. have been used up, as against 35 at Verdun in 5 months. In another 6 weeks, the enemy should be hard put to it to find men.

(*e*) The maintenance of a steady offensive pressure will result eventually in his complete overthrow.

Principle on which we should act. *Maintain our offensive.* Our losses in July's fighting totalled about 120,000 more than they would have been had we not attacked. They cannot be regarded as sufficient to justify any anxiety as to our ability to continue the offensive. It is my intention:

(*a*) To maintain a steady pressure on Somme battle.

(*b*) To push my attack strongly whenever and wherever the state of my preparations and the general situation make success sufficiently probable to justify me in doing so, but not otherwise.

(*c*) To secure against counter-attack each advantage gained and prepare thoroughly for each fresh advance.

Proceeding thus, I expect to be able to maintain the offensive well into the Autumn.

It would not be justifiable to calculate on the enemy's resistance being completely broken without another campaign next year.

Douglas Haig, *Private Papers* (1952), pp.157–8.

Haig's emphasis on relieving France and Russia and on what he liked to call 'wearing down' the enemy inevitably led to much argument about casualty figures. It seems that by the end of the Somme campaign in November German losses were rather higher than those of the Allies, but many British people doubted this at the time, pointing out that the process of 'wearing down' or attrition worked in both directions.

The way in which the war has been understood by later generations has owed much to the memoirs of ex-soldiers such as Sassoon, Blunden and Graves, who wrote in the decade after 1918 with the hindsight and freedom of speech which peace made possible. One of the many 'war books' of that period, H. M. Tomlinson's *All Our Yesterdays* (1930), vividly describes the journey to the Somme battlefield through 'Happy Valley', the last gathering-point before the front line.

> Happy Valley was a desert. Its surface was pulverized by myriads of feet, hooves, and wheels. Restless brown lakes could be seen in it; they were congestions of horses. All the trees of the valley were dead or dying because the horses had gnawed off their bark. A great carnival was being held in the valley; excitement and energy stirred its life, without joy. Its slopes were blotched with the discoloured canvas dwellings of the hands in the new industry of war, surgeons, and craftsmen with rifles and cannon, and their hosts of qualified attendants. The broad valley crawled with humans, cattle, and machinery, and distance merged horses, men and engines into a ceaseless stirring on the hairless hide of the planet. The interest of man had settled on the valley, and had worn it as dead as an ash-pit. From a distance, it was not an army of men you saw there, but merely an eddying of clusters and streams of loose stuff. It was not men, but man-power, which moved into that valley without ceasing, and the power was pumped into it from the reservoirs of distant cities to keep revolving the machinery of war. If life clotted, it was deflected into those hospital tents. The streams had to be constant and free. The flies of all the plagues were in the valley, more flies than men and horses, because every dead man and horse bred an army of flies; the flies darkened the food, shimmered over the ordure, and swarmed on the clotted life in the hospital tents.
> The land around was terraced with massed batteries and howitzers. Their crews laboured at the ranks of glistening steel barrels, stripped to the waist. They fed them glumly and methodically, as in a universal factory where overtime was compulsory for a greater output of death, which nobody wanted. The machinery had

been set going, and the men were its slaves. They could not stop. The engines compelled them to continue as they had begun. They were being broken on the wheels they had started. The wheels and cogs of the age of machines had taken charge of their inventors, and were grinding them and their earth into powder, for the increase of the flies. Work did not finish at sunset. Night was in abeyance. Darkness was an intermittent day; it was tremulous with an incessant flaring and glittering, and the very clouds flushed phantom-like with the red reflections of earth's sinister activities. It was the Battle of the Somme. Giant automata hammered ponderously on the old horizon, breaking it up. The earth sparked and flashed under their poundings. They hammered with a violence so rapid that you knew only soulless bodies of steel could be so powerful and tireless, so blind to ruin, so unheeding of the dismay of listeners. You had a dread that evil had been freed. It was beyond control now, leaping huge malignant rapine over cornlands, orchards, and altars, turning the ancient establishment of prudent peace into dust and corruption.

H. M. Tomlinson, *All Our Yesterdays* (1930), pp.393–5.

Tomlinson records that on the way up to Happy Valley a *John Bull* poster on a barn door bore the words '1916! Thank God!'. His work as one of the first official War Correspondents left him with a lifelong hatred of war and Bottomleyism.

A language very unlike Tomlinson's was used for official regimental histories, as in the following account of the first day of the Somme.

On the morning of July 1st the bombardment of the enemy trenches became intense, but German machine-guns continued to fire from Beaumont-Hamel throughout the bombardment.

At 7.26 a.m., the leading platoons of the assaulting

companies moved out to a line taped-out in 'no-man's-land,' so as to be in line with the 1st Lancashire Fusiliers, of the 29th Division, who were to attack Beaumont-Hamel.

At 7.32 a.m. 'D' Company and Battalion Headquarters followed the attacking companies and established themselves in shell-holes.

A signaller (Lce.-Corpl. J. McDonald, afterwards a Sergeant) accompanied the leading platoon of 'A' Company, carrying a telephone and wire with orders to open communication from German front line, where Battalion Headquarters were to be established.

The personnel of the Headquarters followed up the wire and found the signaller in a large shell-hole just outside the German wire. Of course the wire was cut before it could be used, but the Headquarters remained in the shell-hole until 6 p.m.

Immediately our guns lifted from the German front-line trenches, heavy machine-gun fire was opened from the German front line; from Beaumont-Hamel and Ridge Redoubt, Lieut.-Colonel Green personally counted eight machine-guns firing on the battalion front. Simultaneously the German artillery barrage came down some 200–250 yards in front of our front line and on all assembly trenches.

In spite of this terrific fire, the battalion advanced as steadily as if on manoeuvres until practically the whole battalion became casualties. Actually a few of the leading troops entered and passed the German front-line, but on the front of the right and centre companies the wire was found intact and no way through it could be found. Many men were killed on the wire while attempting to force a way through; among them was Sergeant Redmayne who was shot through the head just as he got out of the trench in front of Colonel Green. Many sought cover in the shell-holes close to the wire which they had vainly attempted to pass.

The survivors of the battalion occupied shell-holes in 'no-man's-land' until they were able to retire to our trenches at dusk. All wounded capable of crawling were sent back first, followed by a rear-guard of unwounded men.

L. Nicholson and H. T. MacMullen, *History of the East Lancashire Regiment in the Great War, 1914–1918* (1936), p.65.

That 'of course' in the fifth paragraph is especially poignant; to find it ironic is to be on the wrong wavelength altogether, for this kind of history is reticent in the same way that soldiers were. The authors were writing mainly for veterans, who could supply from their own memories the colour and detail which print could never convey. The telephone was the only link between advancing troops and their generals, except for runners; it worked as far as the front line because the wire could be buried, but once men entered No Man's Land, with a signaller paying out the wire behind them as they went, shrapnel soon ensured silence. That was typical of a war which took place too soon to be able to make full use of twentieth-century science and engineering. Similarly, troops could reach the war zone quickly by rail, but once they came within range of enemy artillery they could only proceed on foot. The state of technology made it comparatively easy to hold one's ground but murderously difficult to advance. Once the New Armies had climbed over the parapets into the smoke on 1 July 1916, it was many hours before their commanders could discover what had happened to them. The spartan prose of the East Lancashires' historians expresses something of the tragic quality of the Somme.

'An Army Second to None'

The fighting struggled on until November, when objectives that had been marked for capture in July were finally taken. Some help was given by tanks, first used in September, but there were only 36 of them and they proved highly unreliable. Anyone who stands today on Thiepval Ridge with some knowledge of its German defences may be more surprised that it was ever taken than that it resisted for so long. The steep landscape itself, scattered with little cemeteries, seems testimony to the determination of Kitchener's recruits. Churchill, another of the war's historians, concluded that the Somme gained 'no strategic advantage of any kind' except the relief of Verdun, but

> this sombre verdict, which it seems probable posterity will endorse in still more searching terms, in no way diminishes the glory of the British Army. A young army, but the finest we have ever marshalled; improvised at the sound of the cannonade, every man a volunteer, inspired not only by love of country but by a widespread conviction that human freedom was challenged by military and Imperial tyranny, they grudged no sacrifice, however unfruitful, and shrank from no ordeal however destructive. Struggling forward through the mire and filth of the trenches, across the corpse-strewn crater fields, amid the flaring, crashing, blasting barrages and murderous machine-gun fire, conscious of their race, proud of their cause, they seized the most formidable soldiery in Europe by the throat, slew them and hurled them unceasingly backward. If two lives or ten lives were required by their commanders to kill one German, no word of complaint ever rose from the fighting troops. No attack, however forlorn, however fatal, found them without ardour. No slaughter, however desolating, prevented them from returning to the charge. No physical conditions, however severe, deprived their commanders of their obedience and loyalty. Martyrs not less than soldiers, they fulfilled the high purpose of duty with which they were imbued. The battlefields of the Somme were the graveyards of Kitchener's Army. The flower of that generous manhood, which quitted peaceful civilian life in every kind of workaday occupation, which came at the call of Britain, and, as we may still hope, at the call of humanity, and came from the most remote parts of her Empire, was shorn away for ever in 1916. Unconquerable except by

> death, which they had conquered, they have set up a monument of native virtue which will command the wonder, the reverence and the gratitude of our island people as long as we endure as a nation among men.
>
> Winston Churchill, *The World Crisis 1911–1918* (1939 edn), vol.2, pp.1091–2.

That tribute, couched in the Churchillian prose that was to be so effective in the next war, is not from a civilian ignorant of front line conditions. As First Lord of the Admiralty Churchill was obliged to take responsibility for the Gallipoli failure; withdrawing temporarily from politics, he returned to his old job as an Army officer and served in the trenches during the winter of 1915–16. All the same, his rhetoric has gone out of favour; such fine words are considered dangerous because they make war seem heroic, purposeful and worthwhile (as indeed Churchill believed it was). Phrases such as 'glory', 'grudged no sacrifice', 'conscious of their race', 'seized . . . by the throat', and 'Martyrs not less than soldiers', lend to war the glow of religion, racial pride and adventure stories. A modern critic might say that Churchill disguises the actuality of war and that such concealment of the truth can only make future wars more likely.

Whatever one may think about Churchill's salute to the men who fought on the Somme, they had some right to be proud of themselves and to expect recognition. An anonymous writer who was apparently one of their number, calling himself simply 'An Amateur Officer', made claims for them soon afterwards that were as strong as Churchill's.

> We have put an army in the field, composed of civilians, which has held in check, and has defeated, the picked troops of the world, has matched itself against the army which was said to be the greatest, but which was no more than the most highly trained, the most efficiently equipped, and the most unscrupulous in its methods, in the world.

It was thought that England would be an easy prey to these troops of Germany. It was said that the young manhood of our nation was degenerate and decadent, and this charge was repeated by so many and so influential voices that it is small wonder if Germany, at least, believed it true. And England produced an army, second to none that the world has ever seen, an army of volunteers from the counting-house and the plough, the factory and the college, the office and the club; produced it, five million strong, like a mushroom in the mists that are between dark and dawn.

This was England's answer to Germany's sneers at the "contemptible little army of Britain." "Men and more men" have poured in to fill the gaps in the ranks of that great, little army, faster than the German machinery of war, barbarous or otherwise, could make them; so that that little army has never died, has never been beaten, but has grown into an invincible and overwhelming force.

An Amateur Officer, *After Victory* (1917),
pp. 108–9.

'An Amateur Officer' goes on to contrast the State's generous care of the welfare of ordinary soldiers with its earlier neglect of the same men when they had been working-class civilians. He urges, as Churchill often did, that proper provision should be made for the poor in peacetime.

The State, as I have mentioned in an earlier chapter, undertakes to provide all the necessaries of life for its soldier, and for his wife and family, or for his dependents. He has but one thing to do, one thing to live for.

In this present passage of our history, that one thing is a glorious and an honoured thing, as it was honoured never before, a thing which makes him proud and happy, as the State's part of the bargain has made him care-free. In these things we may see why it is that the men who live in the presence of imminent and violent death are happy, constantly happy. It is so much easier to die than to see the children hungry, and to know that food is unobtainable because it belongs to some one else. Is it so surprising, after all, that the wretch from the slum, when he becomes a soldier, becomes also a man?

Will he be treated as a man when he comes home, bringing to us all the gift of victory? Will he be given the chance of remaining a man; or will he go back to his slum? Will his children continue in the slums? Will the children of those who do not come home, who have died for our victory, be left in the slums?

Ibid., pp.166–7.

The disappointing answers to such questions immediately after 1918 were partly responsible for the resentment which many ex-soldiers came to feel about the war, but huge social changes were eventually made. The first moves towards a Welfare State had begun before 1914, but they were given powerful impetus by the sufferings of the troops and by consciences such as that of 'An Amateur Officer'.

'One Must Not Break'

The published records of soldiers' motives and feelings which are still read today are mostly by people of the officer class. It is less easy to find out what the Other Ranks were thinking, although there has recently been valuable research done by means of interviews with survivors. Perhaps the best literary portrait of the troops is that of a small but representative group in Frederic Manning's fine novel, *The Middle Parts of Fortune* (privately printed in 1929, first published in an expurgated version as *Her Privates We* in 1930). Manning was commissioned in 1917, but in 1916 he was still in the ranks, serving as a runner on the Somme. At one stage in the book, in the second half of 1916, members of the platoon discuss their reasons for joining up.

'Chaps,' said Weeper, suddenly, 'for Christ's sake let's pray for rain!'

'What good would that do?' said Pacey, reasonably. 'If they don't send us over the top here, they'll send us over somewhere else. It 'as got to be, an' if it 'as got to be, the sooner it's over an' done wi' the better. If we die, we die, an' it won't trouble nobody, leastways not for long it won't; an' if we don't die now, we'd 'ave to die some other time.'

'What d'you want to talk about dyin' for?' said Martlow, resentfully. 'I'd rather kill some other fucker first. I want to have my fling before I die, I do.'

'If you want to pray, you 'ad better pray for the war to stop,' continued Pacey, 'so as we can all go back to our own 'omes in peace. I'm a married man wi' two children, an' I don't say I'm any better'n the next man, but I've a bit o' religion in me still, an' I don't hold wi' sayin' such things in jest.'

'Aye,' said Madeley, bitterly; 'an' what good will all your prayin' do you? If there were any truth in religion, would there be a war, would God let it go on?'

'Some on us blame God for our own faults,' said Pacey, coolly, 'an' it were men what made the war. It's no manner o' use us sittin' 'ere pityin' ourselves, an' blamin' God for our own fault. I've got nowt to say again Mr Rhys [their officer], 'e talks about liberty, an' fightin' for your country, an' posterity, an' so on; but what I want to know is what all us 'ns are fightin' for. . . .'

'We're fightin' for all we've bloody got,' said Madeley, bluntly.

'An' that's sweet fuck all,' said Weeper Smart. 'A tell thee, that all a want to do is to save me own bloody skin. An' the first thing a do, when a go into t' line, is to find out where t' bloody dressing-stations are; an' if a can get a nice blighty, chaps, when once me face is turned towards home, I'm laughing. You won't see me bloody arse for dust. A'm not proud. A tell thee straight. Them as thinks different can 'ave all the bloody war they want, and me own share of it, too.'

'Well, what the 'ell did you come out for?' asked Madeley.

Weeper lifted up a large, spade-like hand with the solemnity of one making an affirmation.

'That's where th'ast got me beat, lad,' he admitted. 'When a saw all them as didn't know any better'n we did joinin' up, an' a went walkin' out wi' me girl on Sundays, as usual, a just felt ashamed. An' a put it away, an' a put it away, until in th' end it got me down. A knew what it'd be, but it got the better o' me, an' then, like a bloody fool, a went an' joined up too. A were ashamed to be seen walkin' in the streets, a were. But a tell thee, now, that if a were once out o' these togs an' in civvies again, a wouldn't mind all the shame in the world; no, not if I 'ad to slink through all the back streets, an' didn' dare put me nose in t'Old Vaults again. A've no pride left in me now, chaps, an' that's the plain truth a'm tellin'. Let them as made the war come an' fight it, that's what a say.'

'That's what I say, too,' said Glazier [. . . .] 'Why should us'ns fight an' be killed for all them bloody slackers at 'ome? It ain't right. No matter what they say, it ain't right. We're doin' our duty, an' they ain't, an' they're coinin' money while we get ten bloody frong [francs] a week. They don't care a fuck about us. Once we're in the army, they've got us by the balls. Talk about discipline! They don't try disciplinin' any o' them fuckin' civvies, do they? We want to put some o' them bloody politicians in the front line, an' see 'em shelled to shit. That'd buck their ideas up.'

'I'm not fightin' for a lot o' bloody civvies,' said Madeley, reasonably. 'I'm fightin' for myself an' me own folk. It's all bloody fine sayin' let them as made the war fight it. 'twere Germany made the war.'

'A tell thee,' said Weeper, positively, 'there are thousands o' poor buggers, over there in the German lines, as don' know, no more'n we do ourselves, what it's all about.'

'Then what do the silly fuckers come an' fight for?'

asked Madeley, indignantly. 'Why didn' they stay 't 'ome? Tha'lt be sayin' next that the Frenchies sent 'em an invite.'

'What a say is, that it weren't none o' our business. We'd no call to mix ourselves up wi' other folks' quarrels,' replied Weeper.

'Well, I don't hold wi' that,' said Glazier, judicially. 'I'm not fightin' for them bloody slackers an' conchies at 'ome; but what I say is that the Fritzes 'ad to be stopped. If we 'adn't come in, an' they'd got the Frenchies beat, 'twould 'a' been our turn next.'

'Too bloody true it would,' said Madeley. 'An' I'd rather come an' fight Fritz in France than 'ave 'im come over to Blighty an' start bashin' our 'ouses about, same as 'e's done 'ere.'

''e'd never 'ave come to England. The Navy 'd 'ave seen to that,' said Pacey.

'Don't you be too bloody sure about the Navy,' said Corporal Hamley, entering into the discussion at last. 'The Navy 'as got all it can bloody well do, as things are.'

> Frederic Manning, *The Middle Parts of Fortune*
> (1977 reprint of the 1929 text), pp.150–1.

The reader is meant to sense the parallel between this conversation and that among the soldiers in *Henry V* on the eve of Agincourt. The literary reference strengthens the credibility of the characters; Manning's skilful use of dramatic fiction enables the few to speak for the many, as Shakespeare's soldiers do. Weeper sums up his own view after more discussion by saying, ''ere we are, an' since we're 'ere, we're just fightin' for ourselves; we're just fightin' for ourselves, an' for each other'. The loyalty of a soldier to himself and to his immediate comrades, a pattern repeated in every platoon throughout the line, somehow held the Army together. The novel shows that in the end the only motive which survives is that of meeting the personal test which battle imposes on the individual. In the words of the central character, 'one must not break'. Manning believed that it was that test, rather than any larger aim of defending freedom or saving posterity, which prevented soldiers from giving up.

Protest Continues

The small band of civilians who had protested against the war from the outset remained active in 1916, their efforts made more urgent by the need to help 'conscientious objectors' who resisted conscription. (The law was liberal for its time in allowing exemptions on religious and other grounds, but about 1200 men who were not exempted and who refused to undertake war work of any kind were imprisoned; some were harshly treated.) Bertrand Russell, described in the Foreign Office as 'one of the most mischievous cranks in the country', was deprived of his College Fellowship at Trinity, Cambridge, in July 1916 despite protests by many academics, but he refused to be silent. Aware that he was becoming a leader of the opposition to the war, he was energetic in lecturing and publishing. In one of his 1916 books he defined the role of the active pacifist.

> Those who are to begin the regeneration of the world must face loneliness, opposition, poverty, obloquy. They must be able to live by truth and love, with a rational unconquerable hope; they must be honest and wise, fearless, and guided by a consistent purpose. A body of men and women so inspired will conquer – first the difficulties and perplexities of their individual lives, then, in time, though perhaps only in a long time, the outer world. Wisdom and hope are what the world needs; and though it fights against them, it gives its respect to them in the end.
>
> When the Goths sacked Rome, St. Augustine wrote the "City of God," putting a spiritual hope in place of the material reality that had been destroyed. Throughout the centuries that followed St. Augustine's hope lived and gave life, while Rome sank to a village of hovels. For us too it is necessary to create a new hope, to build up by our thought a better world than the

one which is hurling itself into ruin. Because the times are bad, more is required of us than would be required in normal times. Only a supreme fire of thought and spirit can save future generations from the death that has befallen the generation which we knew and loved.

Bertrand Russell, 'What We Can Do', *Principles of Social Reconstruction* (1916), pp.246–7.

Russell goes on to say that the potential leaders of the future, young men of creative energy and hope, were being destroyed, while older men convinced themselves that the sacrifice was necessary, lapsing 'quickly into comfort after any momentary assault of feeling'.

> In such men the life of the spirit is dead. If it were living, it would go out to meet the spirit in the young, with a love as poignant as the love of father or mother. It would be unaware of the bounds of self; their tragedy would be its own. Something would cry out: 'No, this is not right; this is not good, this is not a holy cause, in which the brightness of youth is destroyed and dimmed. It is we, the old, who have sinned; we have sent these young men to the battle-field for our evil passions, our spiritual death, our failure to live generously out of the warmth of the heart and out of the living vision of the spirit. Let us come out of this death, for it is we who are dead, not the young men who have died through our fear of life. Their very ghosts have more life than we: they hold us up for ever to the shame and obloquy of all the ages to come. Out of their ghosts must come life, and it is we whom they must vivify.'

Ibid., p.248.

The traces of D. H. Lawrence in the style and ideas of that passage are not coincidental; Russell's 1916 essays originated in a 1915 plan to give joint lectures with Lawrence. The partnership was short-lived, for the two men soon found themselves in disagreement; the subsequent portrait of Russell

as 'Sir Joshua Malleson' in *Women in Love* shows how alien
Lawrence eventually felt him to be. Lawrence's own position
by the end of 1916 is summed up in his portrait of himself as
Somers in his post-war novel, *Kangaroo*.

> So he discovered the great secret: to stand alone as
> his own judge of himself, absolutely. He took his
> stand absolutely on his own judgement of himself.
> Then, the mongrel-mouthed world would say and do
> what it liked. This is the greatest secret of behaviour:
> to stand alone, and judge oneself from the deeps of
> one's own soul. And then, to know, to hear what the
> others say and think: to refer their judgement to the
> touch-stone of one's own soul-judgement. To fear
> one's own inward soul, and never to fear the outside
> world, nay, not even one single person, nor even fifty
> million persons.
>
> To learn to be afraid of nothing but one's own
> deepest soul: but to keep a sharp eye on the millions
> of the others. Somers would say to himself: 'There are
> fifty million people in Great Britain, and they would
> nearly all be against me. Let them.'
>
> D. H. Lawrence, 'The Nightmare', *Kangaroo*
> (1923), chapter 10.

This sense of extreme isolation was partly caused by the
personal and national effects of conscription; Lawrence was
called up, subjected to a routine medical examination and
rejected as unfit (he was also spied on and banned from living
near the coast). He never forgave the State for these incursions
into his private freedom. For him, as for Russell, conscription
was an assault on human creativity and 'the life of the spirit'.
His disgust is reflected in *Women in Love*, which he began
in April and finished in its first draft during the Somme
fighting; the second draft was complete by November, but
no publisher would accept it. He said he wanted 'the bitterness
of the war' to be 'taken for granted in the characters'
(his portrayal of the mechanical emptiness of contemporary
society was influenced by Mark Gertler's painting, *The
Merry-Go-Round* (Plate 2)).

Although he failed to keep Lawrence as a collaborator, Russell was a hero of the Left by the winter of 1916–17. Among the many people influenced by him were Sassoon, whose 1917 protest was inspired by his ideas and personal advice; Owen, whose 'Strange Meeting' (1918) seems certainly to owe its prophetic, political content to Russell's 1916 essays; and A. G. West, who wrote to him in December 1916.

Tonight here on the Somme I have just finished your *Principles of Social Reconstruction* which I found waiting for me when I came out of the line. . . . It encouraged me all the more as the state of opinion in England seems to fall to lower and lower depths of undignified hatred. It is only on account of such thoughts as yours, on account of the existence of men and women like yourself that it seems worth while surviving the war – if one should haply survive. Outside the small circle of that cool light I can discern nothing but a scorching desert.

Do not fear though that the life of the spirit is dying in us, nor that hope or energy will be spent; to some few of us at any rate the hope of helping to found some 'city of God' carries us away from these present horrors and beyond the graver intolerance of thought as we see it in our papers. We shall not faint and the energy and endurance we have used here on an odious task we shall be able to redouble in the creative work that peace will bring to do. We are too young to be permanently damaged in body or spirit, even by these sufferings.

Rather what we feared until your book came was that we would find no one left in England who would build with us. Remember, then, that we are to be relied on to do twice as much afterwards as we have done during the war, and after reading your book that determination grew intenser than ever; it is for you that we would wish to live on.

I have written to you before and should perhaps apologise for writing again, but that seems to me rather absurd: you cannot mind knowing that you are understood and admired and that those exist who would be glad to work with you.

Arthur Graeme West, letter to Bertrand Russell, 27 September 1916, quoted in Russell, *Autobiography* (1968), vol.2, p.76.

West had little more than three months to live.

5 Dulce et Decorum Est: 1917

Peace Moves and President Wilson

There were political conflicts and demands for peace in many belligerent countries in 1917. Lloyd George was repeatedly challenged to state the Allies' war aims. Suspicion grew that the war now had more to do with trade rivalry than with liberating Europe. In March came news of the Russian Revolution and the abdication of the Czar, events warmly welcomed by British intellectuals. A huge meeting held at the Albert Hall to congratulate Russia heard calls for the end of British rule in Ireland and India, and even for the end of the monarchy. There were Socialist mutinies in Germany and Italy later in the year, but hopes for the fall of the Kaiser were disappointed. The Albert Hall meeting at least showed that free speech was still possible, although occasional clampdowns were causing trouble. Export of *The Nation* was banned in April, officially because the magazine had been exploited by German propaganda but actually because it had called for peace negotiations. Strong objections to the ban were made by Churchill, G. K. Chesterton, Wells, Bennett, Shaw and many others (it was lifted in October). Hints emerged from Germany at various times during the war that negotiations would be welcome, but their reliability was much debated; there was never any clear sign that the German leadership was willing to consider evacuating Belgium.

The American President, Woodrow Wilson, offered to mediate. Speaking to the Senate in January, he said that the United States should work for peace without victory, thereby saving all sides from a legacy of bitterness and humiliation, and for a post-war world led by a league of peace which would ensure freedom on land and sea and a reduction of armaments. Wilson was very much aware of his unique moral position.

Perhaps I am the only person in high authority amongst

123

all the peoples of the world who is at liberty to speak and hold nothing back. I am speaking as an individual, and yet I am speaking also, of course, as the responsible head of a great government, and I feel confident that I have said what the people of the United States would wish me to say. . . .

I am proposing, as it were, that the nations should with one accord adopt the doctrine of President Monroe as the doctrine of the world: that no nation should seek to extend its polity over any other nation or people, but that every people should be left free to determine its own polity, its own way of development, unhindered, unthreatened, unafraid, the little along with the great and powerful.

I am proposing that all nations henceforth avoid entangling alliances which would draw them into competitions of power; catch them in a net of intrigue and selfish rivalry, and disturb their own affairs with influences intruded from without. There is no entangling alliance in a concert of power. When all unite to act in the same sense and with the same purpose all act in the common interest and are free to live their own lives under a common protection.

I am proposing government by the consent of the governed; that freedom of the seas which in international conference after conference representatives of the United States have urged with the eloquence of those who are the convinced disciples of liberty; and that moderation of armaments which makes of armies and navies a power for order merely, not an instrument of aggression or of selfish violence.

These are American principles, American policies. We could stand for no others. And they are also the principles and policies of forward looking men and women everywhere, of every modern nation, of every enlightened community. They are the principles of mankind and must prevail.

Woodrow Wilson, speech to the Senate, 22 January 1917, quoted in H. S. Commager, ed., *Documents of American History* (1942), pp.305–8.

Unfortunately there was not much evidence that these ideas would appeal to the combatants. Instead, Germany decided to resume unrestricted submarine warfare against all shipping supplying the Allies, a move seen by Wilson as 'nothing less than a declaration of war against the government and people of the United States'. In April the President brought American neutrality to an end at last, taking care even so to distance himself from European imperial ambitions and to insist on the morality of America's resolve to 'make the world safe for democracy'.

I have exactly the same things in mind now that I had in mind when I addressed the Senate on the twenty-second of January last. . . . Our object now, as then, is to vindicate the principles of peace and justice in the life of the world as against selfish and autocratic power and to set up amongst the really free and self-governed peoples of the world such a concert of purpose and of action as will henceforth insure the observance of those principles. Neutrality is no longer feasible or desirable where the peace of the world is involved and the freedom of its peoples, and the menace to that peace and freedom lies in the existence of autocratic governments backed by organized force which is controlled wholly by their will, not by the will of their people. We have seen the last of neutrality in such circumstances. We are at the beginning of an age in which it will be insisted that the same standards of conduct and of responsibility for wrong done shall be observed among nations and their governments that are observed among the individual citizens of civilized states.

We have no quarrel with the German people. We have no feeling towards them but one of sympathy and friendship. It was not upon their impulse that their government acted in entering this war. It was not with their previous knowledge or approval. . . .

We are accepting this challenge of hostile purpose because we know that in such a Government, following such methods, we can never have a friend; and that in the presence of its organized power, always lying in wait to accomplish we know not what purpose, there can be no assured security for the democratic Governments of the world. We are now about to accept gauge of battle with this natural foe to liberty and shall, if necessary, spend the whole force of the nation to check and nullify its pretensions and its power. We are glad, now that we see the facts with no veil of false pretence about them, to fight thus for the ultimate peace of the world and for the liberation of its peoples, the German peoples included: for the rights of nations great and small and the privilege of men everywhere to choose their way of life and of obedience. The world must be made safe for democracy. Its peace must be planted upon the tested foundations of political liberty. We have no selfish ends to serve. We desire no conquest, no dominion. We seek no indemnities for ourselves, no material compensation for the sacrifices we shall freely make. We are but one of the champions of the rights of mankind. We shall be satisfied when those rights have been made as secure as the faith and the freedom of nations can make them.

> Woodrow Wilson, speech to Congress, 2 April 1917, ibid., pp.310–11.

The first American troops did not reach France until June, but Wilson's decision put new heart into the Allies. Opponents of the war felt that the chance of peace was now much diminished. In the East the new Russian government continued the war effort. On the Western Front men and munitions poured unceasingly into the swathe of mud and ruin that stretched across Europe, but there seemed to be no end in sight to the fighting.

In France: Owen, Graves, Sassoon

Among the new arrivals in France at the start of 1917 was Wilfred Owen. Well-read in Romantic and Decadent literature, with its persistent themes of death and catastrophe, he was imaginatively attuned to the subject of war, but nothing he had read or heard had given him warning of what the trenches would be like in that bitter winter.

> I can see no excuse for deceiving you about these last 4 days. I have suffered seventh hell.
> I have not been at the front.
> I have been in front of it.
> I held an advanced post, that is, a 'dug-out' in the middle of No Man's Land.
> We had a march of 3 miles over shelled road then nearly 3 along a flooded trench. After that we came to where the trenches had been blown flat out and had to go over the top. It was of course dark, too dark, and the ground was not mud, not sloppy mud, but an octopus of sucking clay, 3, 4, and 5 feet deep, relieved only by craters full of water. Men have been known to drown in them. Many stuck in the mud & only got on by leaving their waders, equipment, and in some cases their clothes.
> High explosives were dropping all around out[side], and machine guns spluttered every few minutes. But it was so dark that even the German flares did not reveal us.
> Three quarters dead, I mean each of us ¾ dead, we reached the dug-out, and relieved the wretches therein. I then had to go forth and find another dug-out for a still more advanced post where I left 18 bombers. I was responsible for other posts on the left but there was a junior officer in charge.
> My dug-out held 25 men tightly packed. Water filled it to a depth of 1 or 2 feet, leaving say 4 feet of air.
> One entrance had been blown in & blocked.
> So far, the other remained.

The Germans knew we were staying there and decided we shouldn't.

Those fifty hours were the agony of my happy life.

Every ten minutes on Sunday afternoon seemed an hour.

I nearly broke down and let myself drown in the water that was now slowly rising above my knees.

Towards 6 o'clock, when, I suppose, you would be going to church, the shelling grew less intense and less accurate: so that I was mercifully helped to do my duty and crawl, wade, climb and flounder over No Man's Land to visit my other post. It took me half an hour to move about 150 yards.

I was chiefly annoyed by our own machine guns from behind. The seeng-seeng-seeng of the bullets reminded me of Mary's canary. On the whole I can support the canary better.

In the Platoon on my left the sentries over the dug-out were blown to nothing. . . . I kept my own sentries half way down the stairs during the more terrific bombardment. In spite of this one lad was blown down and, I am afraid, blinded.

This was my only casualty.

> Wilfred Owen, letter to his mother, 16 January
> 1917, *Poems* (1931).

Months later, Owen used this experience for his poem, 'The Sentry'. His war poems were based on what he saw and felt between January and April 1917, although he did not begin writing them until the autumn. Badly shellshocked in April, he was sent home and was not to return to active service for nearly eighteen months.

Even to soldiers who had been in the trenches in 1915–16 the war seemed more repellent in 1917 than it had done before. Robert Graves was at the huge base camp at Étaples in January.

The instructors at the Bull Ring were full of bullet-and-bayonet enthusiasm which they tried to pass on to the drafts. The drafts were now, for the most part, either forcibly enlisted men or wounded men returning, and at this dead season of the year it was difficult for anyone to feel enthusiastic on arrival in France. The training principle had recently been revised. *Infantry Training*, 1914, had laid it down politely that the soldier's ultimate aim was to put out of action or render ineffective the armed forces of the enemy. This statement was now not considered direct enough for a war of attrition. Troops were taught instead that their duty was to HATE the Germans and KILL as many of them as possible. In bayonet-practice the men were ordered to make horrible grimaces and utter blood-curdling yells as they charged. The bayonet-fighting instructors' faces were permanently set in a ghastly grin. 'Hurt him, now! In at his belly! Tear his guts out!' they would scream as the men charged the dummies. 'Now that upper swing at his privates with the butt. Ruin his chances for life. No more little Fritzes! . . . Naaaoh! Anyone would think that you *loved* the bloody swine, patting and stroking 'em like that. BITE HIM, I SAY! STICK YOUR TEETH IN HIM AND WORRY HIM! EAT HIS HEART OUT!'

Once more I was glad to be sent up to the trenches.

Robert Graves, *Goodbye to All That* (1929),
chapter 21.

Graves proved unfit for further active service, not having fully recovered from the lung wound he had received on the Somme in 1916. He spent the rest of the war in Britain.

Between February and April the Germans carried out a careful plan by moving to a new, stronger trench system, laying the land waste as they retreated. The pursuing British, Sassoon among them, succeeded in penetrating part of the new 'Hindenburg Line' and its deep communication tunnel. Sassoon recorded in his diary that his party set out for the tunnel on 14 April but got lost. *'Things to remember / . . .* stumbling along the trench in the dusk, dead men and living lying against the sides of the trench – one never knew which were dead and which were living. Dead and living were very nearly one, for death was in all our hearts. Kirkby shaking dead German by the shoulder to ask him the way' (*Diaries 1915–1918*, pp.156–7). Five days later, Sassoon combined these incidents in a poem.

> Groping along the tunnel, step by step,
> He winked his prying torch with patching glare
> From side to side, and sniffed the unwholesome air.
>
> Tins, boxes, bottles, shapes too vague to know;
> A mirror smashed, the mattress from a bed;
> And he, exploring fifty feet below
> The rosy gloom of battle overhead.
>
> Tripping, he grabbed the wall; saw some one lie
> Humped at his feet, half-hidden by a rug,
> And stooped to give the sleeper's arm a tug.
> 'I'm looking for headquarters.' No reply.
> 'God blast your neck!' (For days he'd had no sleep,)
> 'Get up and guide me through this stinking place.'
> Savage, he kicked a soft, unanswering heap,
> And flashed his beam across the livid face
> Terribly glaring up, whose eyes yet wore
> Agony dying hard ten days before;
> And fists of fingers clutched a blackening wound.
>
> Alone he staggered on until he found
> Dawn's ghost that filtered down a shafted stair
> To the dazed, muttering creatures underground
> Who hear the boom of shells in muffled sound.
> At last, with sweat of horror in his hair,
> He climbed through darkness to the twilight air,
> Unloading hell behind him step by step.
>
> Siegfried Sassoon, 'The Rear-Guard' (final draft),
> *The Old Huntsman and Other Poems* (1917).

A decade or more afterwards Sassoon returned to these memories, this time telling the story in the laconic prose of

George Sherston, the straightforward, unpoetic character he invented as his counterpart in his three volumes of fictionalised memoirs (*Memoirs of a Fox-Hunting Man*, 1928; *Memoirs of an Infantry Officer*, 1930; *Sherston's Progress*, 1936).

The Tunnel was a few inches higher than a tall man walking upright; it was fitted with bunks and recessed rooms; in places it was crowded with men of various units, but there were long intervals of unwholesome-smelling solitude. Prying my way along with an electric torch, I glimpsed an assortment of vague shapes, boxes, tins, fragments of broken furniture and frowsy mattresses. It seemed a long way to Headquarters, and the Tunnel was memorable but not fortifying to a fatigued explorer who hadn't slept for more than an hour at a stretch or taken his clothes off since last Tuesday. Once, when I tripped and recovered myself by grabbing the wall, my tentative patch of brightness revealed somebody half hidden under a blanket. Not a very clever spot to be taking a nap, I thought as I stooped to shake him by the shoulder. He refused to wake up, so I gave him a kick. "God blast you, where's Battalion Headquarters?" My nerves were on edge; and what right had he to be having a good sleep, when I never seemed to get five minutes' rest? . . . Then my beam settled on the livid face of a dead German whose fingers still clutched the blackened gash on his neck. . . . Stumbling on, I could only mutter to myself that this was really a bit too thick. (That, however, was an exaggeration; there is nothing remarkable about a dead body in a European War, or a squashed beetle in a cellar.) At Headquarters I found the Adjutant alone, worried and preoccupied with clerical work.

Siegfried Sassoon, *Memoirs of an Infantry Officer*
(1930), viii.5.

The differences between these two versions of the original events illustrate some of the differences between Sassoon and Sherston; readers often forget that the protagonist is not the same man as his creator.

Seeing It Through

The spring offensive in 1917 was led by the French, with a disastrous assault on the Aisne. The British gave wasted support at Arras, where Edward Thomas was killed among many others. French troops mutinied and for a while the British had to take the strain in the West. Things looked bleak.

Worried by 'defeatism' and 'peace talk' at home, Churchill called on the countrymen of Mr Britling to 'see it through' with undimmed resolve.

> Hopes are excited in credulous minds that the message of the Russian revolution leaping across the lines of the armies, and the measured pronouncements of the President of the United States reverberating across the oceans, will awaken a responsive echo in the hard heart of the German nation. It is hoped that the masses of the German people, taught by their own sufferings, taught by the counsel of America, the opinion of the world and the example of the Russian democracy, will by a single spontaneous effort free themselves from the cruel and terrible machine which galls them and forces them to gall mankind. Sanguine dreamers, moving nimbly in the attenuated ether of ideas, can almost see the German nation, master at last in its own house, decreeing the liberation of imprisoned nationalities, directing the reparation of the ravaged regions, breaking the sword that torments them and us alike, and confidently taking their own great place among the free nations of the world. But the soaring flight of such ideas is abruptly checked by contact with reality.

> Winston Churchill, 'Final Chapters of the Great War / The Task Before Us – We Have Got to Hold On', *Sunday Pictorial*, 20 May 1917.

The reality, Churchill said, was that Germany was still determined on victory, and the German people were not about to revolt. The Allies had 'GOT TO HOLD ON' in the confidence that their new strength on land and their immense superiority at sea would prove decisive once the Americans had become established.

> Sure of this, Mr Britling will not waver. He will look back to the true and pure and disinterested feelings with which he began this war. He will make sure that he seeks nothing which divorces him from contact with those feelings: he will make sure that he accepts nothing that does not fully satisfy those feelings. He will banish from his mind all temptations of booty or revenge. He will equally repel all thought of compromise with evil. He will concentrate his whole mind and soul upon the essential and irrevocable purpose for which his son and other dear ones yielded up their lives – namely, the dethronement from its bad pre-eminence of that system of lust and cunning backed by force and armed with science, which for want of a better name, or a worse, the civilised and humane nations of the world have learned to call 'Prussian Militarism'.
>
> Thus Mr Britling will be able to say, not, alas! to his own gallant son, but in a happier generation to his daughter's child, '*I saw it through*'.

> Ibid.

Marking the beginning of the fourth year, *The Times* repeated the case against Germany which it had set out in 1914 (see above, p.34), dismissed German peace moves and concluded that the struggle was more than ever one of good against evil. The newspaper's determination was in line with that of Lloyd George and the Government.

> The battle is still a battle for our existence and our honour, for the safety of our Empire and our shores, for all our most elementary possessions as a people. But not less is it still a battle for our highest conceptions of right and for our loftiest aspirations in politics. It is today, more manifestly than at any time before, a

battle between good and evil, between law and brute force, between freedom and tyranny, between democracy and despotism. We have shed our best blood in torrents and lavished our accumulated wealth in thousands of millions to safeguard our interests and to vindicate justice, liberty, and truth. We are not going to make these sacrifices vain by accommodation or by compromise with the enemy who pursues our ruin that he may trample on the sacred principles we guard.

The Times, leading article, 4 August 1917.

Passchendaele

The second half of 1917 brought what is often thought of as the archetypal 'battle' of the war. The Third Battle of Ypres, commonly known as Passchendaele, lasted from July to November. Long afterwards, a survivor speaking on a radio programme described Passchendaele as one of the British Army's greatest feats of arms. The troops floundered for months over ground which heavy rain and shelling soon turned into a nightmare of deep mud, but they eventually captured the village of Passchendaele. Even so, the objective proved impossible to hold. This costly and apparently futile offensive gave rise to more resentment and cynicism in the ranks than had been felt before. Haig always believed that the campaign had been necessary, but he was bitterly criticised for it later, especially by his arch-enemy, Lloyd George.

And now we come to the battle which, with the Somme and Verdun, will always rank as the most gigantic, tenacious, grim, futile and bloody fights ever waged in the history of war. Each of these battles lasted for months. None of them attained the object for which they were fought. In each case it was obvious early in the struggle to every one who watched its course – except to those who were responsible for the strategic plan that wrought the grisly tragedy – that the goal would not be reached. Taken together they were responsible for the slaughter or mutilation of between 2,000,000 and 3,000,000 of brave men. The tale of these battles constitutes a trilogy illustrating the unquenchable heroism that will never accept defeat and the inexhaustible vanity that will never admit a mistake. It is the story of the million who would rather die than own themselves cowards – even to themselves – and also of the two or three individuals who would rather the million perish than that they as leaders should own – even to themselves – that they were blunderers. Hence the immortal renown and the ghastly notoriety of the Verdun, Somme and Passchendaele battlefields; the fame won by sustained valour unrivalled in the annals of war; the notoriety attained by a narrow and stubborn egotism, unsurpassed amongst the records of disaster wrought by human complacency.

Falkenhayn, Joffre, and Haig were trained soldiers who had worked hard to master their profession. But there is no profession where experience and training count less in comparison with judgment and flair. The intervals between great wars are fortunately so considerable, and in this age of restless invention the change in mechanism and therefore in methods is also so considerable and so rapid, that imagination, resource, initiative and flexibility are more essential to success in the vocation of the soldier than in any other.

The battle of the Flanders mud, better and more bitterly known as the Battle of Passchendaele, had been put into Sir Douglas Haig's tenacious brain as early as 1916. If it failed it was not for lack of the most elaborate and prolonged preparations. In July, 1917, he told the War Cabinet that he had been preparing for it the whole year.

David Lloyd George, *War Memoirs* (1938), vol.2, p.1247.

Whatever may be said about Haig, there was certainly an ironic contrast between conditions at the front and life in the charming old town which his Staff had taken over as their headquarters, as one of the official War Correspondents, Philip Gibbs, later recalled.

> I came to know G.H.Q. more closely when it removed for fresher air to Montreuil, a fine old walled town, once within sight of the sea, which ebbed over the low-lying ground below its hill, but now looking across a wide vista of richly cultivated fields where many hamlets are scattered among clumps of trees. One came to G.H.Q. from journeys over the wild desert of the battle-fields, where men lived in ditches and "pill-boxes," muddy, miserable in all things but spirit, as to a place where the pageantry of war still maintained its old and dead tradition. It was like one of those pageants which used to be played in England before the War, picturesque, romantic, utterly unreal. It was as though men were playing at war here, while others, sixty miles away, were fighting and dying, in mud and gas-waves and explosive barrages.
>
> An "Open Sesame," by means of a special pass, was needed to enter this City of Beautiful Nonsense. Below the gateway, up the steep hillside, sentries stood at white posts across the road, which lifted up on pulleys when the pass had been examined by a military policeman in a red cap. Then the sentries slapped their hands to their rifles to the occupants of any motor car, sure that more staff-officers were going in to perform those duties which no private soldier could attempt to understand, believing they belonged to such mysteries as those of God. Through the narrow streets walked elderly generals, middle-aged colonels and majors, youthful subalterns all wearing red hatbands, red tabs, and the blue-and-red armlet of G.H.Q., so that colour went with them on their way.
>
> Often one saw the Commander-in-Chief starting for an afternoon ride, a fine figure, nobly mounted, with two A.D.C.'s and an escort of Lancers. A pretty sight, with fluttering pennons and all their lances, and horses groomed to the last hair. It was prettier than the real thing up in the Salient or beyond the Somme,

where dead bodies lay in upheaved earth among ruins and slaughtered trees. War at Montreuil was quite a pleasant occupation for elderly generals who liked their little stroll after lunch, and for young Regular officers. . . .

The smart society of G.H.Q. was best seen at the Officers' Club in Montreuil, at dinner-time. It was as much like musical comedy as any stage setting of war at the Gaiety. A band played ragtime and light music while the warriors fed, and all these generals and staff officers, with their decorations and arm-bands and polished buttons, and crossed swords, were waited upon by little W.A.A.C.'s with the G.H.Q. colours tied up in bows on their hair. Such a chatter! such bursts of light-hearted laughter! such whisperings of secrets and intrigues and scandals in high places! such careless-hearted courage when British soldiers were being blown to bits, gassed, blinded, maimed and shell-shocked in places that were far – so very far – from G.H.Q.!

Philip Gibbs, *Realities of War* (1920), pp.25–7.

It was necessary for GHQ to be well out of enemy artillery range, but the insensitivity of 'chateau generalship' was bound to cause resentment. Too many senior officers seemed entirely unaware of the sufferings of the troops, often making their miseries worse by a perverse insistence on Army regulations. To take one typical example, men going into the trenches were required to paint or otherwise obscure equipment that might give away their position by reflecting sunlight, but sometimes everything had to be polished up again afterwards.

Spit and polish is the order of the day, and I am all for it – in reason. But when the men have just come out, after sixteen days in the line, where they have been squeezed up in muddy dug-outs during the few hours in the daytime when they were not on duty and could get a sleep – for they stand to all night, I think it is a bit thick when high-placed officers, who do not share their dangers and discomforts, and indeed never, or scarcely ever, go into the firing line, kick up Hell's delight because the bayonet scabbards are not polished! Yet such is the kind of thing we had sometimes to put up with from our friends behind the front.

Personally, I prefer the attentions of our enemies. These are at least logical, and so think all the front line. Although, during the sixteen days and nights the battalion has been up, the breastworks have been collapsed by the rains – to say nothing of German shells and trench-mortars; though our patrols have nightly explored Noman's Land and the German wire, not a word is said about that. Not a remark. Not a comment. It is *polished* bayonet scabbards that they want. The real business we are here for is not even referred to. Can you believe it?

Rowland Feilding, *War Letters to a Wife* (1929), pp.224–5.

Passchendaele began on 31 July 1917. One survivor, Bernard Martin, remembered his experience of that day vividly enough to be able to write about it in his ninetieth year. His task had been to lead his men across No Man's Land to a German trench which the Staff had named Jehovah.

I spaced my men along the tape evenly, one metre or so apart. Shells from our barrage screeched just over our heads. The enemy artillery, taken by surprise, had not yet opened fire. I set a steady walking pace, everything going according to plan. But after a few steps I found myself in a huddle on the ground, gasping for breath, bewildered. The blast of a shell had thrown me down violently. As I struggled to get up, to regain balance, still confused, I realised that what seemed to be an unrecognisable heap on the ground alongside me was, in fact, a man; one arm extended, a long bare arm disclaiming any connection with the body, the hand open with fingers wide apart as though glad to be done with grasping. Undoubtedly a Goner. I'd seen many such empty bodies with that general appearance of having been thrown away in a hurry, no longer wanted. When I regained my balance and my composure, I saw several gaps in our line: casualties. Could only be from a 'short-fall', one of our own shells, what the Artillery called 'short rounds'. I'd never worried about 'short-falls' before, they landed in the open when we were below ground in trenches, but it was bad luck to have one at the very start of our walk-over attack. Almost at once we had another . . . shrapnel . . . bursting low. Notwithstanding the solid noise of the barrage, I could pick out the zip-zip of metal fragments whizzing past my ears. A third 'short-fall' killed my sergeant and two men. The situation was serious. We were about halfway to Jehovah and a third of our strength already casualties. The mind works so much faster than the body acts. I found my thoughts debating why so many short-falls: can it be that a big concentration of guns on a short front also concentrates the short-falls? Surely that would have been foreseen by whoever planned this battle? No time for theories, the light was now strong enough to see what damage our gunners had done to Jehovah. I glanced at my watch. In a few moments we must make our charge at the double.

My reflections were cut short. From the battered parapet of Jehovah, a little to my left, I saw the flash of a rifle: so we could expect some resistance. Another rifle flash, this one straight in front . . . a knock-out blow . . . legs sagging . . . collapse: and as I crossed the hazy limits of consciousness into the non-world, I knew I had been shot through the head.

*   *   *

How long in that same fit I lay,
I have not to declare:
But ere my living life return'd,
I heard, and in my soul discerned
Two voices in the air.

I hope it's not presumption for an Ancient Warrior

to borrow a few words of immortal poetry. Coleridge's Mariner was telling a story with a moral; my fragment of autobiography has no moral and is merely an account of war as experienced by one common-or-garden infantry subaltern. But my last experience was so fantastic that the facts can do with a hint of poetry to help them snuggle down alongside Truth.

I saw a rifle fired point-blank in my direction as I was walking towards Jehovah trench, felt a knock-out blow, knew I'd been hit in the head, that my legs were giving way, my body collapsing, my mind surrendering consciousness. These facts were registered in less time than they take to tell, but it's not sufficient merely to say, 'I was there and I saw it.' Between dawn and dusk on the 31st July, 1917 I was sometimes *not* there. How long I lay in the first fit of total unconsciousness I do not know. Thereafter, I drifted in and out of varied degrees of consciousness; sometimes eyes closed, my mind wayward as in a dream, at other times wide-eyed and as clear-thinking as I've ever been. Such was my last experience of war, 'a mighty sum of things forever speaking', in my memory [. . . .]

A sound outside my mind stirred me to fresh awareness – two voices in the air. I opened my eyes (astonished to discover that my eyes had not been shot away). I lay on the rim of a shell hole. Two men, at a lower level, were staring up at me, on the ground between them a stretcher. Of course – stretcher-bearers, gleaning the battlefield, collecting wounded who'd been overlooked in the first harvest. Strong men, tough chaps, accustomed to horror-sights, to mutilations and handling the half-dead. No use for me. I wasn't worth gleaning. I wanted to shoo them away, to shout, 'For God's sake go away, my number's up and I'm content', but I could not speak, or make any sound, or so much as raise a warning hand. I was as helpless as any decaying corpse on any battlefield. But I could hear, my ears still worked.

'Poor bugger looks like he's a Goner.'

'Saw his eyes flicker.'
'Waste o' time I reckon. Take off his waterbottle,
put it where 'e can reach it if 'e wants a drink.'
''Ow the 'ell could 'e drink with that face? You
lookin' for a bloody miracle?'

> Bernard Martin, *Poor Bloody Infantry* (1987),
> pp.160–4.

Martin had been hit through cheek and jaw by a fragment of
shrapnel, probably British. Finding himself suddenly under
shellfire, he managed to walk back to the trenches and was
eventually invalided out of the Army with 'twenty per cent
permanent disability'. It is noteworthy that what saved his
life was the fear of being shelled. Enduring heavy shelling
with no chance of escape was the worst ordeal of all, reducing
the strongest men to uncontrollable trembling and ultimately
nervous collapse. As Martin repeatedly points out, the 'poor
bloody infantry' did very little actual fighting, being usually
nothing more than the passive victims of distant artillery.
Despite the intense terror felt by almost all soldiers before
'going over the top', men often felt relief and even euphoria
during the subsequent advance across No Man's Land.

> Our division had the task of attacking Passchendaele.
> None of us knew where to go when the barrage began,
> whether half left or half right. A vague memory of
> following the shellbursts as long as the smoke was
> black, and halting when it changed to white came to
> me. The whole affair appeared rather good fun. You
> know how excited one becomes in the midst of danger.
> I forgot absolutely that shells are meant to kill and not
> to provide elaborate lighting effects. I looked at the
> barrage as something provided for our entertainment –
> a mood of madness if you like. A fat builder loaded
> with 500 rounds acted the brave man, ran on ahead,
> signalled back to us as if on a quiet parade. The last I
> saw of him was two arms straining madly at the
> ground, blood pouring from his mouth while legs and
> body sank into a shellhole filled with water. One

Highlander, raving mad, shouted at us. 'Get on you cowards. Why don't you run at them?' . . . an aeroplane swooped down and treated us to a flood of bullets. I never enjoyed anything so much in my life – flames, smoke, SOSs, lights, drumming of guns, swishing of bullets all appeared stage properties to set off a majestic scene. From the pictorial view, nothing could be finer. It had a unity of colour and composition all of its own. The most delicate shades of grey and green and brown fused wonderfully in the opening light of the morning. I confess my first feelings of deadly fear only arose first when lying wounded on a stretcher. The first excitement was wearing off and my teeth were chattering with the cold. Shrapnel was drumming overhead down the line of the duckboard track. Nothing frightens one more than high shrapnel for the bullet strikes the head first. With high explosive one can lie down or side-slip . . .

M. Quigley, quoted in Denis Winter, *Death's Men* (1978), pp.180–1.

There is a memorable description of the opening stages of Third Ypres in Edmund Blunden's *Undertones of War* (1928). Blunden narrowly escaped death in the early stages of the engagement, while sheltering with some fellow officers in a former German pill-box.

Presently the drizzle was thronging down mistily again, and shelling grew more regular and searching. There were a number of concrete shelters along the trench, and it was not hard to see that their dispossessed makers were determined to do them in. Our doctor, an Irishman named Gatchell, who seemed utterly to scorn such annoyances as Krupp, went out to find a much discussed bottle of whisky which he had left in his medical post. He returned, the bottle in his hand; "Now, you toping rascals" – a thump like a thunderbolt stopped him. He fell mute, white, face down, the bottle still in his hand; "Ginger" Lewis, the unshakable Adjutant, whose face I chanced to see particularly, went as chalky-white, and collapsed; the Colonel, shaking and staring, passed me as I stooped to pull the doctor out, and tottered, not knowing where he was going, along the trench. This was not surprising. Over my seat, at the entrance, the direct hit had made a gash in the concrete, and the place was full of fragments and dust. The shell struck just over my head, and I suppose it was a 5.9. But we had escaped, and outside, scared from some shattered nook, a number of fieldmice were peeping and turning as though as puzzled as ourselves. A German listening-set with its delicate valves stood in the rain there, too, unfractured. But these details were perceived in a flash, and meanwhile shells were coming down remorselessly all along our alley. Other direct hits occurred. Men stood in the trench under their steel hats and capes, resigned to their fate.

Edmund Blunden, *Undertones of War* (1928), chapter 21.

It was characteristic of Blunden, a nature poet in a hideously unnatural landscape, to notice and remember the mice. They recur in his poetic version of the same incident.

> At the noon of the dreadful day
> Our trench and death's is on a sudden stormed
> With huge and shattering salvoes, the clay dances
> In founts of clods around the concrete sites,
> Where still the brain devises some last armour
> To live out the poor limbs.
> This wrath's oncoming
> Found four of us together in a pillbox,
> Skirting the abyss of madness with light phrases,
> White and blinking, in false smiles grimacing.
> The demon grins to see the game, a moment
> Passes, and – still the drum-tap dongs my brain
> To a whirring void – through the great breach above
> me
> The light comes in with icy shock and the rain

Horridly drips. Doctor, talk, talk! if dead
Or stunned I know not; the stinking powdered con-
crete,
The lyddite turns me sick – my hair's all full
Of this smashed concrete. O I'll drag you, friends,
Out of the sepulchre into the light of day,
For this is day, the pure and sacred day.
And while I squeak and gibber over you,
Look, from the wreck a score of field-mice nimble,
And tame and curious look about them; (these
Calmed me, on these depended my salvation).

Edmund Blunden, 'Third Ypres', *The Shepherd,
and Other Poems of Peace and War* (1922), ll.83–105.

Immediately after this, Blunden was asked to send assistance
to a far worse disaster, where a shell had hit forty or more of
his colleagues. Helping other soldiers was a more urgent
necessity than defeating the Germans, who were no doubt
suffering just as much. Blunden carried the burden of his
front-line experiences for the rest of his life.

Still wept the rain, roared guns,
Still swooped into the swamps of flesh and blood,
All to the drabness of uncreation sunk,
And all thought dwindled to a moan, Relieve!
But who with what command can now relieve
The dead men from that chaos or my soul?

Ibid., ll.120–5.

Blunden's prose and verse about the war were mostly written
in the twenties. They are memorials to the suffering and
endurance of his former companions, whom he remembered
with profound, tormented affection. If *Undertones of War*
and its associated poems can be regarded, as they often are,
as protests against the war, they are less direct in their
protesting than the wartime work of Sassoon, Barbusse or
Owen.

Soldiers Protest: Sassoon, Barbusse, Owen

Despite conditions at the front, and ʼ impetus given to Socialism by events in Russia, protests by British soldiers *during and against* the war were very much rarer than is often supposed. Most complaints were of the kind regularly aired in *John Bull*'s 'Tommy and Jack' column, which printed grouses from soldiers and sailors about food, inefficiency, low pay, corruption and so on. Even that column was technically illegal, since members of the armed forces, like other Crown servants, were forbidden to criticise the conduct of the war, but it seems unlikely that fear of the law was the main reason for the general lack of protest. The denunciation of the war itself which Sassoon composed in June 1917 seems to have been unique. He sent copies to his commanding officer, Hardy, Bennett, Carpenter, Wells, Russell, Graves, the editor of *The Nation*, and various public personages, including an MP who read it out in the House of Commons.

I am making this statement as an act of wilful defiance of military authority, because I believe that the War is being deliberately prolonged by those who have the power to end it. I am a soldier, convinced that I am acting on behalf of soldiers. I believe that this War, upon which I entered as a war of defence and liberation, has now become a war of aggression and conquest. I believe that the purposes for which I and my fellow-soldiers entered upon this War should have been so clearly stated as to have made it impossible for them to be changed without our knowledge, and that, had this been done, the objects which actuated us would now be attainable by negotiation.

I have seen and endured the sufferings of the troops, and I can no longer be a party to prolonging those sufferings for ends which I believe to be evil and unjust.

I am not protesting against the military conduct of the War, but against the political errors and insincerities for which the fighting men are being sacrificed.

On behalf of those who are suffering now, I make

this protest against the deception which is being practised on them. Also I believe that it may help to destroy the callous complacence with which the majority of those at home regard the continuance of agonies which they do not share, and which they have not sufficient imagination to realise.

Siegfried Sassoon, public statement, *The Times*, 31 July 1917.

Sassoon found surprisingly little support. His backers were civilians, notably Russell, whose opinions are reflected in his first paragraph. Soldiers seem to have been unimpressed. His comrades wrote to him from the front, saying the war had to go on. His friend and fellow officer, Graves, pressed for him to be diagnosed as 'neurasthenic' or shellshocked, telling him that protests merely lowered morale in the trenches without affecting the politicians. Sassoon was undoubtedly showing signs of severe mental strain. The authorities decided to send him to Craiglockhart War Hospital, letting him know that he would remain there until he agreed to be quiet. It was an ingenious and comparatively humane solution, rendering his protest ineffective but saving him from court martial and possibly from breakdown. In the long run, however, the attempt to silence him was to have quite the reverse effect; while he was in hospital he not only wrote many of the poems that were to appear in his *Counter-Attack and Other Poems* (1918) but also met and encouraged another patient, Wilfred Owen.

Sassoon showed Owen the poems he was working on. Although he was an introspective lyrical poet by inclination, he had become adept since 1916 at satirising civilian complacency.

Does it matter? – losing your legs? . . .
For people will always be kind,
And you need not show that you mind
When the others come in after hunting
To gobble their muffins and eggs.

Does it matter? – losing your sight? . . .
There's such splendid work for the blind;
And people will always be kind,
As you sit on the terrace remembering
And turning your face to the light.

Do they matter? – those dreams from the pit? . . .
You can drink and forget and be glad,
And people won't say that you're mad;
For they'll know that you've fought for your country
And no one will worry a bit.

> Siegfried Sassoon, 'Does It Matter?', *The Cambridge Magazine*, 6 October 1917.

Owen was much impressed by this kind of writing and was quick to imitate it. Sassoon gave him typically Georgian advice about the importance of sincerity, simplicity of language and truth to experience; he also lent him books, including *Under Fire*.

Under Fire (1917), the English translation of Henri Barbusse's *Le Feu* (1916), was one of the most outspoken protests so far available. Writing from experience and as a fervent Communist, Barbusse told the symbolic, harrowing story of a squad of French soldiers. Like Russell, Sassoon and *The Labour Leader*, he believed that the troops were being duped by the ruling class. Rhetoric about the glory of war was a device for exploiting and deceiving worker soldiers. *Under Fire* ends with an exhortation to the men in the ranks to identify and remember their oppressors, and then with a final scene of soldiers lying in the mud.

> "They will say to you," growled a kneeling man who stooped with his two hands in the earth and shook his shoulders like a mastiff, 'My friend, you have been a wonderful hero!' I don't *want* them to say it!
> "Heroes? Some sort of extraordinary being? Idols? Rot! We've been murderers. We have respectably followed the trade of hangmen. We shall do it again

with all our might, because it's of great importance to
follow that trade, so as to punish war and smother it.
The act of slaughter is always ignoble; sometimes
necessary, but always ignoble. Yes, hard and persistent
murderers, that's what we've been. But don't talk to
me about military virtue because I've killed Germans."

"Nor to me," cried another in so loud a voice that
no one could have replied to him even had he dared;
"nor to me, because I've saved the lives of Frenchmen!
Why, we might as well set fire to houses for the sake
of the excellence of life-saving!"

"It would be a crime to exhibit the fine side of war,
even if there were one!" murmured one of the sombre
soldiers.

The first man continued. "They'll say those things
to us by way of paying us with glory, and to pay
themselves, too, for what they haven't done. But
military glory – it isn't even true for us common
soldiers. It's for some, but outside those elect the
soldier's glory is a lie, like every other fine-looking
thing in war. In reality, the soldier's sacrifice is
obscurely concealed. The multitudes that make up the
waves of attack have no reward. They run to hurl
themselves into a frightful inglorious nothing. You
cannot even heap up their names, their poor little
names of nobodies."

"To hell with it all," replies a man, "we've got other
things to think about."

"But all that," hiccupped a face which the mud
concealed like a hideous hand, "may you even *say* it?
You'd be cursed, and 'shot at dawn'! They've made
around a Marshal's plumes a religion as bad and stupid
and malignant as the other!"

The man raised himself, fell down, and rose again.
The wound that he had under his armour of filth was
staining the ground, and when he had spoken, his
wide-open eyes looked down at all the blood he had
given for the healing of the world.

Henri Barbusse, *Under Fire* (1917), pp.340–1.

Barbusse's arguments and passionate conviction had a powerful effect on Sassoon, whose diary contains very similar ideas,
and on Owen, several of whose poems, including 'Dulce et
Decorum Est', echo phrases in the book.

Owen wrote 'Dulce et Decorum Est' in October.

> Bent double, like old beggars under sacks,
> Knock-kneed, coughing like hags, we cursed through
>   sludge,
> Till on the haunting flares we turned our backs
> And towards our distant rest began to trudge.
> Men marched asleep. Many had lost their boots
> But limped on, blood-shod. All went lame; all blind;
> Drunk with fatigue; deaf even to the hoots
> Of tired, outstripped Five-Nines that dropped behind.
>
> Gas! GAS! Quick, boys! – An ecstasy of fumbling,
> Fitting the clumsy helmets just in time;
> But someone still was yelling out and stumbling,
> And flound'ring like a man in fire or lime . . .
> Dim, through the misty panes and thick green light,
> As under a green sea, I saw him drowning.
>
> In all my dreams, before my helpless sight,
> He plunges at me, guttering, choking, drowning.
>
> If in some smothering dreams you too could pace
> Behind the wagon that we flung him in,
> And watch the white eyes writhing in his face,
> His hanging face, like a devil's sick of sin;
> If you could hear, at every jolt, the blood
> Come gargling from the froth-corrupted lungs,
> Obscene as cancer, bitter as the cud
> Of vile, incurable sores on innocent tongues,–
> My friend, you would not tell with such high zest
> To children ardent for some desperate glory,
> The old Lie: Dulce et decorum est
> Pro patria mori.

Wilfred Owen, Poems (1920).

The Roman ideal summed up in the famous Latin saying ('It

is sweet and decorous to die for the fatherland') had been
esteemed and taught to children for centuries; Owen's rejec-
tion of it marks a decisive and apparently permanent change
in literary and social values. His poetry did not bring about
the change but it has strongly reinforced it.

Owen originally addressed his poem to Jessie Pope, a
popular versifier whose effusions in the Right-wing press
frequently glorified war and soldiers ('They'll take the Kaiser's
middle wicket / And smash it by clean British Cricket'). It
was not only civilians, however, who believed that dying for
the fatherland was indeed 'dulce et decorum'.

If England calls to-day –
   The last long call of all,
   Valhalla's Trumpet-call:
   Then may I live until
   The Goal shines past the Hill
   And in the last grand rally
   Hear echoed God's Reveille
       In the Home Camp.

If England calls this day –
   If in the great, grim fight
   I fall – with eyes all bright
   With sacrificial flame
   Whispering Her great name:
   Let these weak verses show
   To all the friends I know –
       I gladly died.

     Harold John Jarvis, 'Dulce et Decorum Est Pro
     Patria Mori', *The Poetry Review*, February 1917.

The author of this poem was an infantry corporal who had
presumably been in the trenches. 'Soldier-poetry' like his
enjoyed a considerable vogue in 1915–17, when hundreds of
amateur poets appeared in print.

Bottomleyism

Corporal Jarvis no doubt meant what he said. There was no such excuse for Horatio Bottomley, who frequently claimed in public that death in war ensured personal salvation and that Britain was leading the world to heaven on earth; in private he was cynical about religion, admitting that he was using it for political and commercial purposes. However, Bottomley did believe that Germany had to be destroyed; unconvinced that the Government shared his determination, he was as much a protester as Sassoon, although his aims were entirely different. Allowed to visit the front in 1917, he wrote articles about his tour for weeks afterwards. 'MORE TRUTH FROM THE TRENCHES – What Haig Told Me – A Message for Lloyd George – Wonderful Tommy!', he announced in one such report. He had asked Haig to let him see

> some good fighting. I told him I wanted to see the men on both sides charging each other with bayonets; our cavalry in full pursuit; I wanted to see trenches and dug-outs blown into the air – woods in flames; Huns throwing down their arms and surrendering, prisoners marching through by the thousand into the cages; bombs dropping everywhere from the air – 'and generally,' said I, 'something like real war, as I understand it'.
>
> Horatio Bottomley, *John Bull*, 29 September 1917.

It was by this sort of statement that Bottomley tried to persuade his soldier readers that he knew what war was like; many newspaper articles still preferred to avoid mention of violence. Haig failed to provide him with any entertainment, so he went to a hospital and came back with a message for the Prime Minister.

> I have come from the Front with a special message for the Prime Minister. It has been given by officers

of all ranks, and by the men in their thousands – aye, and by men lying terribly wounded in hospital. On Tuesday, Sept. 11th, I sat at the bedside of a dying soldier. His wounds were too pitiful to behold. He had recognised me and had asked the nurse to bring me to him. It was in the Canadian Hospital (which means that the hospital is staffed by Canadian doctors and nurses – there is no distinction in nationality of the patients at these glorious institutions). I went to the poor fellow, spoke words of comfort – and I hope of Love – to him, and leant over his wan and pain-racked face to catch his weakening whispers. 'Don't let them patch it up,' were almost his last words. Well, I bring that message to Mr Lloyd George – as head of the King's Government. 'Remember that the Asquith declaration, made when you were a member of his Ministry, and more than once endorsed by you, pledged us to fight on "until the military domination of Prussia is fully and *finally destroyed*". In other words, we are out to slay the Teutonic Military monster, and the place to slay him in is Berlin – so that the German people may see it die, and know that it *is* dead. I ask you to declare at once emphatically that this is still the "aim' of Britain. Let there be no ambiguity about it. The boys at the Front demand it. And don't have any more of those ridiculous Paris Conferences [to discuss a negotiated peace]. Believe me, the fighting men have something better to do. When they have got the Hun on his knees, pleading for peace – then, and not till then, will be your turn. But you must make one condition precedent – *peace must be discussed in Berlin*. That is the message I bring from the Trenches. Heed it.'

Ibid.

The story of the dying man should not be dismissed as fiction, although Bottomley was perfectly capable of inventing it. Many soldiers still wanted complete victory and were uneasy that civilian timidity might persuade the politicians to make a premature peace. Bottomley and other journalists encouraged such thinking, thereby helping to set up hopelessly unrealistic expectations. *John Bull*'s readers were led to believe that Germany could and should be destroyed and at the same time be made to pay the Allies' costs in full, that soldiers would earn rich rewards on earth as in heaven, and that peace would bring perfect happiness. Whether or not the troops were duped by the ruling class, most of whom probably regarded Bottomley with disgust, some of them were certainly duped by what Lawrence called 'that bloated ignominy, *John Bull*' (see above, p.85).

Lord Lansdowne's Letter

It was a member of the ruling class who made what was perhaps the most influential and publicised call for peace moves. In November *The Daily Telegraph* published a long letter from Lord Lansdowne (architect of the *Entente Cordiale* and Conservative Foreign Secretary, 1900–5, and Minister in the Coalition, 1915–16). Lansdowne accepted that the war was being fought for European security, but said it had already gone far enough.

> We are not going to lose this war, but its prolongation will spell ruin for the civilised world, and an infinite addition to the load of human suffering which already weighs upon it. Security will be invaluable to a world which has the vitality to profit by it, but what will be the value of the blessings of peace to nations so exhausted that they can scarcely stretch out a hand with which to grasp them?
>
> In my belief, if the war is to be brought to a close in time to avert a world-wide catastrophe, it will be brought to a close because on both sides the peoples of the countries involved realise that it has already lasted too long.
>
> There can be no question that this feeling prevails extensively in Germany, Austria, and Turkey. We know beyond doubt that the economic pressure in

those countries far exceeds any to which we are subject here. Ministers inform us in their speeches of the 'constant efforts' on the part of the Central Powers 'to initiate peace talks'.

Lord Lansdowne, letter, *The Daily Telegraph*,
29 November 1917.

Lansdowne went on to suggest that the vagueness of the peace offers made by the Central Powers might be a result of the severe limits to free speech in Germany and of the misrepresentation of Allied war aims by German propagandists. The German people had been told that the Allies wanted to ruin Germany, end her commercial power, impose a puppet government and take control of her shipping. With the skill of an experienced politician Lansdowne thus attributed to enemy propaganda views which had in fact frequently been expressed in Britain. He urged the Government to deny holding any such war aims, pointing out that this would be of great assistance to the peace movement in Germany. Not surprisingly, his letter was greeted with outrage by newspapers such as *John Bull* and *The Daily Express*, but it was warmly welcomed in other quarters. What *was* the war being fought for? The pacifists had been asking that question since 1914; Sassoon's protest had repeated it; and now a respected elder statesman had raised it with diplomatic force in a Conservative newspaper. Public concern might have been greater still if it had been known that Lansdowne had expressed his views to the Cabinet a year earlier, warning that war by attrition was 'slowly but surely killing off the best male population of these islands'.

1917 ended with a little good news from the battlefronts. 324 tanks went into action at Cambrai with enough success for bells to be rung for the first time in the war, although the gains were rapidly equalled by losses. The British force in the Middle East, which had been advancing for most of the year after recovering from earlier disasters, captured Jerusalem. It was hardly enough to still doubting voices at home. A far more momentous event had occurred in the autumn, when the

Russian Bolsheviks under Lenin and Trotsky had overthrown Kerensky's moderate government. Russia stopped fighting in the middle of December. Free at last to subdue her Eastern Front, Germany could now concentrate her forces in the West.

6 Retreat and Victory: January–November 1918

War Aims

1918 started quietly. On 5 January the Prime Minister outlined Allied war aims to a meeting of trade unionists. He insisted that the war was being fought for democracy, but warned that if Russia chose to make a separate peace the Allies would be unable to save her from Prussian domination. He also emphasised that they were not waging a war of aggression against Germany, nor had they any wish to destroy Germany's commerce or constitution, although they naturally hoped that the German people would opt for democracy once the conflict was over. While not rejecting all possibility of a negotiated peace, he said that German peace proposals so far had been much too vague. Germany still wanted her colonies back and had not offered to evacuate Belgium. The Allied principle for all peoples was government with the consent of the governed, and there was little chance that any territory would consent to revert to German rule. A peace treaty would have to be binding and an international body would have to be set up to make peace endure.

So long as the possibility of dispute between nations continues, that is to say, so long as men and women are dominated by passioned ambition, and war is the only means of settling a dispute, all nations must live under the burden not only of having from time to time to engage in it, but of being compelled to prepare for its possible outbreak. The crushing weight of modern armaments, the increasing evil of compulsory military service, the vast waste of wealth and effort involved

156

in warlike preparation, these are blots on our civilisation of which every thinking individual must be ashamed.

For these and other similar reasons, we are confident that a great attempt must be made to establish by some international organisation an alternative to war as a means of settling international disputes. After all war is a relic of barbarism, and, just as law has succeeded violence as the means of settling disputes between individuals, so we believe that it is destined ultimately to take the place of war in the settlement of controversies between nations.

If, then, we are asked what are we fighting for, we reply, as we have often replied: We are fighting for a just and a lasting peace, and we believe that before permanent peace can be hoped for three conditions must be fulfilled.

First, the sanctity of treaties must be re-established; secondly, a territorial settlement must be secured based on the right of self-determination or the consent of the governed; and, lastly, we must seek by the creation of some international organisation to limit the burden of armaments and diminish the probability of war.

In these conditions the British Empire would welcome peace, to secure those conditions its peoples are prepared to make even greater sacrifices than those they have yet endured.

> David Lloyd George, *War Memoirs* (1938), vol.2,
> pp.1516–17.

These sentiments were designed to please the Prime Minister's trade union audience and beyond it President Wilson, several of whose cherished aims and phrases he was careful to echo. A comparison with Asquith's September 1914 speech (p.57 above) may suggest why Bottomley and others were worried that the Government was now too soft. Lloyd George seemed to give no grounds for the doubts expressed by Russell, Sassoon and others, and implied by Lansdowne, that Britain was fighting for 'aggression and conquest'. Instead of attacking 'Prussianism', he spoke of self-government and government by consent, with implications not only for the territories claimed or occupied by Germany or being captured from Turkey, but also for British colonies (Britain had recently given autonomy to the Dominions and begun to appoint native administrators in India). A League of Nations, once only an intellectuals' dream, was now Government policy.

Behind the scenes politicians and generals schemed against one another in their attempts to shape policy and strategy. The extent of these machinations only became public after the war, when memoirs began to appear. One of the more notorious records was the diary of Colonel Repington, who had the ear of many influential people and the entry into many great houses. Repington was a busy campaigner in support of victory on the Western Front, sharing the suspicion held by other 'Westerners' that Lloyd George was deliberately starving Haig of men in the hope of securing a compromise peace before more slaughter could occur. He was adept at using the newspapers to reveal secret information which would embarrass the Government, coming close to treason on occasions. His note of a conversation with Haig (now a Field Marshal) soon after Lloyd George's speech to the unions shows something of the ill-feeling that existed between the Prime Minister and the Commander-in-Chief in this period of approaching crisis.

> The F.M. was very critical of our conduct of the war, saying that we should either make war or make peace. L.G. has been to see him when he, L.G., was being criticised, and had practically accused him of inciting journalists against the Government. This accu-sation he had vehemently repudiated. He had asked the P.M. to name one journalist incited. The P.M. named S., whereupon Haig said that he would write to him, but the P.M. begged him not to do so. L.G. threatened a counter-offensive, and asked Haig what he would say if he, L.G., described Haig's offensive as useless slaughter when he spoke at the Guildhall, and if he said that the men had been smothered in mud and blood. Haig answered that he would consider such

a speech to be highly unpatriotic, and then went on to tell me that the spirit of an Army was a delicate plant, and would not remain uninfluenced at last by the constant attacks against its leaders. He said that if L.G. did not like his, Haig's, leading he should remove him.

The F.M. asked me what I thought the Boche would do. I said I supposed that he would attack as Haig had sketched out, but that the concentration in the West was, after all, natural, and might fit in with an intention to stand in a strong attitude if peace negotiations began, as the civilian element in Germany obviously desired. H. is due to appear before the War Cabinet to-morrow, and asked me what they were thinking and whether they were much alarmed about the position. I said that I thought that they were sufficiently alarmed, and that L.G.'s speech yesterday to the Labour Unions, with the throwing over of Russia and the closer approach to the Boche peace ideas, showed it. But I said that if we alarmed them too much we should get a weak compromise peace and all would have to be begun again later. After all, we had as many Boche divisions against us last spring, when we were taking the offensive, as we had now, though how many more there were to come up was another matter.

C. à C. Repington, *The First World War 1914–1918* (1920), vol.2, p.174.

The debate about war aims was vigorously pursued by the leading commentators on the war, among whom, needless to say, was H. G. Wells. Wells said that modern warfare was so hideous and all-embracing that mankind was no longer safe anywhere without world peace. Peace could be achieved either by international co-operation, which was now an Allied aim, or by allowing one state to dominate all the others, which was 'manifestly the ambition of the present rulers of Germany'.

Whatever the complications may have been in the

earlier stages of the war, due to treaties that are
now dead letters and agreements that are extinct, the
essential issue now before every man in the world is
this: Is the unity of mankind to be the unity of a
common freedom, in which every race and nationality
may participate with complete self-respect, playing its
part, according to its character, in one great world
community, or is it to be reached – and it can only be
so reached through many generations of bloodshed
and struggle still, even if it can be ever reached in
this way at all – through conquest and a German
hegemony?

While the rulers of Germany to-day are more openly
aggressive and imperialist than they were in August,
1914, the Allies arrayed against them have made great
progress in clearing up and realizing the instincts and
ideals which brought them originally into the struggle.
The German government offers the world to-day a
warring future in which Germany alone is to be secure
and powerful and proud. *Mankind will not endure
that.* The Allies offer the world more and more
definitely the scheme of an organized League of Free
Nations, a rule of law and justice about the earth. To
fight for that and for no other conceivable end, the
United States of America, with the full sympathy and
co-operation of every state in the western hemisphere,
has entered the war. The British Empire, in the midst
of the stress of the great war, has set up in Dublin a
Convention of Irishmen of all opinions with the fullest
powers of deciding upon the future of their country.
If Ireland were not divided against herself she could
be free and equal with England to-morrow. It is the
open intention of Great Britain to develop representative government, where it has not hitherto existed, in
India and Egypt, to go on steadfastly increasing the
share of the natives of these countries in the government
of their own lands, until they too become free and
equal members of the world league. Neither France
nor Italy nor Britain nor America has ever tampered
with the shipping of other countries except in time of

war, and the trade of the British Empire has been impartially open to all the world. The extra-national "possessions," the so-called "subject nations" in the Empires of Britain, France, Italy, and Japan, are, in fact, possessions held in trust against the day when the League of Free Nations will inherit for mankind.

> H. G. Wells, 'The War Aims of the Western Allies', *In the Fourth Year* (1918), pp.81–3.

Wells went on to challenge the German people to choose between the alternatives he had posed, but concluded gloomily that the Allies were still not speaking plainly.

> In such terms as these the Oceanic Allies could now state their war-will and carry the world straightway into a new phase of human history. They could but they do not. For alas! not one of them is free from the entanglements of past things; when we look for the wisdom of statesmen we find the cunning of politicians; when open speech and plain reason might save the world, courts, bureaucrats, financiers and profiteers conspire.

> Ibid., p.84.

Disgust at the intrigue and dishonesty that seemed dominant in public life was not limited to wayward non-combatants such as Wells. Sassoon had given up his protest in December and gone out again to be with the troops, saying that looking after his men was the only worthwhile thing left for him to do. Men returning from the front on leave were angered by what they saw as the luxury and hypocrisy of life in Britain. It was a divide which peace would not be able to heal.

Officer and Conscripts

The Army now contained great numbers of young conscripts, many of them under twenty. Bewildered, scarcely trained and often unsuited to the tasks demanded of them, they needed all the help that experienced officers and NCOs could give. The hero of Ford Madox Ford's novel, *No More Parades*, Christopher Tietjens, is responsible for a large draft of men at a base camp in France early in 1918, getting them ready to go into the line.

> Intense dejection: endless muddles: endless follies: endless villainies. All these men given into the hands of the most cynically care-free intriguers in long corridors who made plots that harrowed the hearts of the world. All these men toys: all these agonies mere occasions for picturesque phrases to be put into politicians' speeches without heart or even intelligence. Hundreds of thousands of men tossed here and there in that sordid and gigantic mud-brownness of mid-winter . . . by God, exactly as if they were nuts wilfully picked up and thrown over the shoulder by magpies. . . . But men. Not just populations. Men you worried over there. Each man a man with a backbone, knees, breeches, braces, a rifle, a home, passions, fornications, drunks, pals, some scheme of the universe, corns, inherited diseases, a greengrocer's business, a milk walk, a paper stall, brats, a slut of a wife. . . . The Men: the Other Ranks!

> Ford Madox Ford, *No More Parades* (1925),
> p.19.

The entanglement of duties faced by a competent officer in 1918 is evoked in a scene at the camp. A junior colleague has challenged Tietjens to write a sonnet, giving him the rhymes (those for the octave are 'Death, moil, coil, breath, saith, oil, soil, wraith'). Another officer, Hotchkiss, is nervously trying to get out of taking a draft up the line, so Tietjens has to tell him how to find a substitute. Outside the hut, the Sergeant-Major is assembling the men.

> The voice of Sergeant-Major Cowley exclaimed tranquilly from outside:
> 'Fall in now. Men who've got their ring papers and

identity disks – three of them – on the left. Men who
haven't, on the right. Any man who has not been able
to draw his blankets tell Colour-Sergeant Morgan.
Don't forget. You won't get any where you're going.
Any man who hasn't made his will in his Soldier's
Small Book or elsewhere and wants to, to consult
Captain Tietjens. Any man who wants to draw money,
ask Captain Mackenzie. Any R.C. who wants to go
to confession after he has got his papers signed can
find the R.C. padre in the fourth hut from the left in
the Main Line from here. . . . And damn kind it is of
his reverence to put himself out for a set of damn
blinking mustard-faced red herrings like you [. . . .
What] good they as asks for you thinks you'll be out
there God knows. You *look* like a squad of infants'
companions from a Wesleyan Sunday school. That's
what you look like and, thank God, we've got a Navy.'
   Under cover of his voice Tietjens had been writing:
   'Now we affront the grinning chops of *Death*,' and
saying to Lieutenant Hotchkiss: 'In the I.B.D. ante-
room you'll find any number of dirty little squits of
Glamorganshires drinking themselves blind over *La
Vie Parisienne.* . . . Ask any one of them you
like. . . .' He wrote:

And in between our carcass and the *moil*
Of marts and cities, toil and moil and *coil.* . .

'You think this difficult!' he said to Mackenzie.
'Why, you've written a whole undertaker's mortuary
ode in the rhymes alone,' and went on to Hotchkiss:
'Ask anyone you like as long as he's a P.B. officer. . . .
Do you know what P.B. means? No, not Poor
B——y, Permanent Base. Unfit . . . If he'd like to take
a draft to Bailleul.'
   The hut was filling with devious, slow, ungainly
men in yellow-brown. Their feet shuffled desultorily;
they lumped dull canvas bags along the floor and held
in unliterary hands small open books that they dropped
from time to time. From outside came a continuing,
swelling and descending chant of voices; at times it

would seem to be all one laugh, at times one menace, then the motives mingled fugally, like the sea on a beach of large stones. It seemed to Tietjens suddenly extraordinary how shut in on oneself one was in this life. . . . He sat scribbling fast: 'Old Spectre blows a cold protecting *breath* . . . Vanity of vanities, the preacher *saith* . . . No more parades, Not any more, no *oil* . . .' He was telling Hotchkiss, who was obviously shy of approaching the Glamorganshires in their ante-room . . . 'Unambergris'd our limbs in the naked *soil* . . .' that he did not suppose any P.B. officer would object. They would go on a beanfeast up into the giddy line in a first-class carriage and get draft leave and command pay too probably . . . 'No funeral struments cast before our wraiths . . .' 'If any fellow does object, you just send his name to me and I will damn well shove it into extra orders. . . .' [. . . . He] scribbled the rapid sestet to his sonnet which ought to make a little plainer what it all meant. Of course the general idea was that, when you got into the line or near it, there was no room for swank: typified by expensive funerals. As you might say: No flowers by compulsion . . . No more parades! . . .

Ibid., pp.50–3.

Ford shows the technical skills that might be expected from an author who had collaborated with Conrad and influenced the Imagists before the war. The layers of activity and language are adroitly handled, the formality of the poem interweaving with the tired clichés of Army speech and the unceasing movement of Tietjens' thoughts. The sonnet, its phrasings grotesquely out of place in their wartime setting, contains the gist and title of the novel. 'No more parades': the war has ended the old world of ceremony, order and degree. Even the old language is out of date. The once-honourable values of Tory England, on which Tietjens' life had been based, are now only relics of the past; instead, there are the masses, pouring into the hut, with their need for welfare and discipline. The scene is an image of the alterations in social concerns which the war helped to bring about. The four Tietjens novels, known collectively as *Parade's End (Some Do Not*, 1924; *No More Parades*, 1925; *A Man Could Stand Up*, 1926; *Last Post*, 1928), form an impressive study of the change and decay in British society in the war period.

The German March 1918 Offensive

Although Tietjens could see no end to the routine of slaughter in early 1918, the rigidity of trench warfare was soon to break. The first two months of the year were one of those times when the newspapers liked to report 'All quiet on the Western Front', a phrase which exasperated the men in the trenches, but on the other side of Europe Germany was making enormous gains. 'Things look stupefyingly catastrophic on the Eastern Front,' Owen said in a February letter, adding that a friend of his thought the whole of civilisation was 'extremely liable to collapse'. Once the Germans had conquered in the East, they would go for that 'knock-out blow' which the Allies had tried and failed to deliver in 1916 and 1917. It might well succeed. Allied troops were weary and there were few reserves. R. C. Sherriff's play *Journey's End*, first performed in 1928, is set in a British dug-out before St Quentin in March 1918. The original audience would have remembered all too vividly the significance of that place and date, knowing from the start that the characters were doomed. The officer in charge orders his men to put barbed wire all round their position; their only task is to fight until they are wiped out. Sherriff did not exaggerate. The German assault came on 21 March, less than two weeks after the Russians had accepted crushing peace terms. An immense barrage along forty miles of the British front destroyed the trench network within hours. The breakthrough was worst at St Quentin. Whole battalions vanished, never to be heard of again. The daily casualty rate for the next few weeks was to be the highest of the war, much higher even than the Somme or Passchendaele. Survivors of the Somme saw the ground they had so slowly won being rapidly lost. The chance for peace negotiations, if it had ever existed, was now over.

Russell admitted privately that opponents of the war had a duty to try to stop a runaway horse but not a runaway express train. Sassoon, both in June and years later, said that the resurgence of German aggression meant that only war could end war. The 'Prussianists' in Britain, of whom there were many, felt themselves vindicated; there had never been any point in dreaming of peace without victory, because Germany was, and always had been, determined to follow Bernhardi's advice, 'World-power or downfall'. In the Press, the language and spirit of 1914 returned, as the nation nerved itself to face the disaster.

By April things were so desperate that the Allies finally had to accept a unified Western Command under the French General, Foch. On the 12th the British Commander-in-Chief issued his 'backs to the wall' order to all ranks, 'a stern call to duty and death,' as Conan Doyle described it, 'pitched on the very note which would arouse the historic tenacity of the British soldier'.

Three weeks ago today the enemy began his terrific attacks against us on a fifty-mile front. His objects are to separate us from the French, to take the Channel ports, and destroy the British Army.

In spite of throwing already 106 divisions into the battle, and enduring the most reckless sacrifice of human life, he has, as yet, made little progress towards his goals. We owe this to the determined fighting and self-sacrifice of our troops.

Words fail me to express the admiration which I feel for the splendid resistance offered by all ranks of our army under the most trying circumstances.

Many amongst us now are tired. To these I would say that victory will belong to the side which holds out the longest.

The French Army is moving rapidly and in great force to our support.

There is no other course open to us but to fight it out. Every position must be held to the last man: there must be no retirement. With our backs to the wall, and believing in the justice of our cause, each one of us must fight to the end.

The safety of our homes and the freedom of mankind depend alike upon the conduct of each one of us at this critical moment.

> Field Marshal Sir Douglas Haig, Order to All
> Ranks, 12 April 1918.

These rallying words were followed by similar calls in the newspapers. Laurence Binyon was one of several leading civilian poets to 'do his bit' by contributing a poem.

> Naked reality, and menace near
> As fire to scorching flesh, shall not affright
> The spirit that sees, with danger-sharpened sight,
> What it must save or die for; not the mere
> Name, but the thing, now doubly, trebly dear,
> Freedom; the breath those hands would choke; the
>   light
> They would put out; the clean air they would blight,
> Making earth rank with hate, and greed, and fear.
>
> Now no man's loss is private: all share all.
> Oh, each of us a soldier stands to-day,
> Put to the proof and summoned to the call;
> One will, one faith, one peril. Hearts, be high,
> Most in the hour that's darkest! Come what may,
> The soul in us is found, and shall not die.

> Laurence Binyon, 'The Test', *The Four Years*
> (1919).

This sonnet appeared (untitled) on 15 April in *The Times*, where many patriotic poems had received their first publication. Being owned by Lloyd George's ally, Lord Northcliffe, *The Times* was always ready to print material that might help to stiffen the nation's morale.

Owen, Aldington, Read

The crisis of spring 1918 is now remembered less vividly than the campaigns of 1916–17. This may partly be because the authors of the most frequently read 'war books' have little to say about it; for example, Graves was out of the fighting, Blunden was sent home just before the March Offensive, and Sassoon was in Palestine. Of the few poets left on the Western Front, Rosenberg was killed on 1 April, but Herbert Read survived the retreat, later describing it in a vivid prose account ('In Retreat', 1925) and in a sequence of short Modernist poems ('The Scene of War', 1919).

The strongest literary response to the disaster came from Owen, who was sent on a physical training course near Ripon at the end of March, when the Army was preparing every available man for the front, even convalescents who might under other circumstances have remained on home duties. Knowing he had little time, Owen rented a cottage room as a place to work in. Here he wrote or revised many of his war poems, following Wordsworth's practice of composing from 'emotion recollected in tranquillity' by deliberately reviving the sensations and experiences of his 1917 trench service, a courageous undertaking for a man who had only recently recovered from severe shellshock. His most famous poem, 'Strange Meeting', is Ripon work and seems to sum up his reflections on the March fighting. Although he never completed his plans for a book, his rough notes for a Preface survive (words which he cancelled are shown here in square brackets).

This book is not about heroes. English Poetry is not yet fit to speak of them.
Nor is it about [battles, and glory of battles or lands, or] deeds or lands nor anything about glory or honour any might, majesty, dominion or power [whatever] except War.
[Its This book] is Above all I am not concerned with Poetry.

[Its The] My subject is War, and the pity of [it] War.
The Poetry is in the pity.

[I have no hesitation in making public
                              publishing such]
[My] Yet These elegies are [not for the consolation]
to this generation in no sense consolatory to this [a
bereaved generation]. They may be to the next. [If I
thought the letter of this book would last, I woul
might have used proper names;] All a poet can do
today is [to] warn [children] That is why the true
[War] Poets must be truthful.

If I thought the letter of this book would last, I
[wo] might have used proper names: but if the spirit
of it survives – survives Prussia – [I] my ambition and
those names will [be content; for they] have achieved
[themselves ourselves] fresher fields than Flanders,
                    far be, not of war
                                        would be
              sing
      Wilfred Owen, draft of a Preface, Spring 1918.

Owen never gave up hope that his poetry would arouse 'pity',
in the future if not in his own time.
    Other writers were less constructive. One of the least
hopeful books about the war, Richard Aldington's *Death of
a Hero*, has its closing scenes on the 1918 battlefields. The
fighting in France went against the Allies for many weeks,
men struggling to survive among the wreckage of nearly four
years of shelling.

The days passed into weeks, the weeks into months.
He moved through impressions like a man hallucina-
ted. And every incident seemed to beat on his brain
Death, Death, Death. All the decay and death of
battlefields entered his blood and seemed to poison
him. He lived among smashed bodies and human
remains in an infernal cemetery. If he scratched his

stick idly and nervously in the side of a trench, he
pulled out human ribs. He ordered a new latrine to
be dug out from the trench, and thrice the digging had
to be abandoned because they came upon terrible black
masses of decomposing bodies. At dawn one morning
when it was misty he walked over the top of Hill 91,
where probably nobody had been by day since its
capture. The heavy mist brooded about him in a
strange stillness. Scarcely a sound on their immediate
front, though from north and south came the vibration
of furious drum-fire. The ground was a desert of shell-
holes and torn rusty wire, and everywhere lay skeletons
in steel helmets, still clothed in the rags of sodden
khaki or field grey. Here a fleshless hand still clutched
a broken rusty rifle; there a gaping, decaying boot
showed the thin, knotty foot-bones. He came on a
skeleton violently dismembered by a shell explosion;
the skull was split open and the teeth lay scattered on
the bare chalk; the force of the explosion had driven
coins and a metal pencil right into the hip-bones and
femurs. In a concrete pill-box three German skeletons
lay across their machine-gun with its silent nozzle still
pointing at the loop-hole. They had been attacked
from the rear with phosphorous grenades, which burn
their way into the flesh, and for which there is no
possible remedy. A shrunken leather strap still held a
battered wrist-watch on a fleshless wrist-bone. Alone
in the white curling mist, drifting slowly past like
wraiths of the slain, with the far-off thunder of drum-
fire beating the air, Winterbourne stood in frozen
silence and contemplated the last achievements of
civilized men.

Richard Aldington, *Death of a Hero* (1929),
III.18.

Few of the war novels published in the twenties give a more
savage account of Army and home life in 1914–18 than *Death
of a Hero*. The humanity of the 'hero', George Winterbourne,
is relentlessly destroyed. Civilian attitudes ruin his domestic

life, while Army service reduces him to an automaton. In the
end he commits suicide – by standing up. There was a kind
of heroism in such a death; the permanent stoop that was
necessary for survival at the front seemed an image of man's
humiliation (hence the title of Ford's novel about the end of
the war, *A Man Could Stand Up*).

Winterbourne is a fictional character, broken by a combination of circumstances crueller than the lot of the average
soldier. A less extreme case of disillusion can be followed in
Herbert Read's 1917–18 letters. As a scholarly philosopher,
whose political thinking owed much to Marx and Nietzsche,
Read was himself far from being an average subaltern, but he
felt like Brooke before going into action, 'extraordinarily
calm and happy'.

> I'm not exactly a warrior by instinct – I don't glory
> in fighting for fighting's sake. Nor can I say that I'm
> wildly enthusiastic for 'the Cause'. Its ideals are a bit
> too commercial and imperialistic for my liking. And I
> don't really hate the Hun – the commonest inspiration
> among my comrades. I know there are a lot of nasty
> Huns – but what a lot of nasty Englishmen there are
> too. But I think my gladness may be akin to that
> Rupert Brooke expressed in one of his sonnets:
>
>> Now God be thanked who has match'd us with His
>>   hour,
>>   And caught our youth, and wakened us from
>>   sleeping,
>> With hand made sure, clear eye, and sharpen'd
>>   power,
>>   To turn, as swimmers into cleanness leaping,
>> Glad from a world grown old and cold and weary,
>>   Leave the sick hearts that honour could not move,
>> And half-men, and their dirty songs and dreary,
>>   And all the little emptiness of love.
>
> Though I must say I'm not yet so 'fed up' with the
> world as the sonnet implies. I haven't yet proved 'the
> little emptiness of love'. The half-men I still have with
> me in goodly numbers. And I've still faith that there

are hearts that can be moved by honour and ideals. But England of these last few years has been rather cold and weary, and one finds little left standing amid the wreckage of one's hopes. So one is glad to leap into the clean sea of danger and self sacrifice. But don't think that I am laying claim to a halo. I don't want to die for my king and country. If I do die, it's for the salvation of my own soul, cleansing it of all its little egotisms by one last supreme egotistic act.

> Herbert Read, *The Contrary Experience* (1963),
> pp.89–90.

(Read quotes from 'Peace', one of Brooke's *1914* sonnets.) What makes this passage interesting is not only that it was written in April 1917, two years after Brooke's death, but also that Read had been in the trenches before. The notion that Brooke-like gladness was never expressed after the Somme, especially by men who knew what the front was like, is manifestly inaccurate; Read's comments are also a reminder that at the core of Brooke's feelings was something much more like egotism than patriotism. However, Read was in a different frame of mind by October 1917, though still repelled by the 'coldness' of England.

We have had a terrible time – the worst I have ever experienced (and I'm getting quite an old soldier now). Life has never seemed quite so cheap nor nature so mutilated. I won't paint the horrors to you. Some day I think I will, generally and for the public benefit. I was thoroughly 'fed up' with the attitude of most of the people I met on leave – especially the Londoners. They simply have no conception whatever of what war really is like and don't seem concerned about it at all. They are much more troubled about a few paltry air raids. They raise a sentimental scream about one or two babies killed when every day out here hundreds of the very finest manhood 'go west'. Of course, everyday events are apt to become rather monotonous . . . but if the daily horror might accumulate we should have such a fund of revulsion as would make the world cry 'enough!' So sometimes I wonder if it is a sacred duty after all 'to paint the horrors'.

Ibid., p.112.

That 'sacred duty to "paint the horrors"' was the poetic task to which Owen and Sassoon were already devoting themselves at Craiglockhart. Read's poetry in that winter was similarly intended as an attack upon civilian rhetoric and ignorance. In March 1918 his unit was among those directly in the path of the enemy advance. The worst was over by May when he summed up his latest thinking.

> How sick I am of the whole business. Most of the prisoners we took were boys under twenty. Our own recent reinforcements were all boys. Apart from uniforms, German and English are as like as two peas: beautiful fresh children. And they are massacred in inconceivable torment. This is the irony of this war: individually we are the one as good as the other: you can't hate these innocent children simply because they dress in grey uniforms. And they are all magnificently brave, English and German alike. But simply because we are united into a callous inhuman association called a State, and because a State is ruled by politicians whose aim (and under the circumstances their duty) is to support and maintain the life and sovereignty of this monster, life and hope are denied and sacrificed. And look at their values. On the one hand national well-being and vanity, commercial expansion, power: on the other love, joy, hope – all that makes life worth living – all that persuades one to consent to live among so much that is barbarous and negative.

Ibid., p.128.

Unlike Winterbourne, Read emerged from his ordeal with steady nerves. His affection for the troops and scorn for politics were like Sassoon's, except that he added his own anarchism. Here, then, is an example of a poet who went into battle quoting Brooke and came out as 'sick of the whole business' as Sassoon. It is often assumed that most soldier poets emerged from the trenches similarly convinced that they were being exploited by the State and politicians, but other examples are hard to find in documents written at the time. The many hundreds of poems written by soldiers in the later stages of the war often express resentment at civilian attitudes and hatred of war, but they rarely call for peace without victory and almost never envisage defeat. Read himself went on fighting, although in later life he became an active pacifist, joining Russell in London demonstrations.

The Final Months

The German advance slowed down and was eventually reversed. Both Haig and Foch mounted successful counter-attacks. No one on the Allied side was fully aware of how weak Germany had become after four years of being blockaded. The British public, having come close to despair, was slow to realise that the war might actually be nearing its end. On 8 August a combined Allied offensive marked what Ludendorff, the German Commander-in-Chief, called 'the black day of the German Army'. C. E. Montague watched the advance from a high point near Amiens, feeling that victory had come too late.

> Troops might only have gained a few hundred yards in the old Flanders way, and then flopped down to dig and be murdered. Or – but one kept a tight hand on hope. One had hoped too often since Loos. And then the mist lifted. It rolled right up into the sky in one piece, like a theatre curtain, almost suddenly taking its white quilted thickness away from between our eyes and the vision so much longed for during four years. Beyond the river a miracle – *the* miracle – had begun. It was going on fast. Remember that all previous advances had gained us little more than freedom to skulk up communication trenches a mile or two further eastward, if that. But now! Across the

level Santerre, which the sun was beginning to fill with
a mist-filtered lustre, two endless columns of British
guns, wagons, and troops were marching steadily east,
unshelled, over the ground that the Germans had held
until dawn.

Nothing like it had ever been seen in the war.
Above, on our cliff, we turned and stared at each
other. We must have looked rather like Cortes' men
agape on their peak. The marvel seemed real; the road
lay open and dry across the Red Sea. Far off, six
thousand yards off in the shining south-east, tanks and
cavalry were at work, shifting and gleaming and looking
huge on the sky-line of some little rumpled fold of the
Santerre plateau. Nearer, the glass could make out an
enemy battery, captured complete, caught with the
leather caps still on the muzzles of guns. The British
dead on the plain, horses and men, lay scattered thinly
over wide spaces; scarcely a foundered tank could be
seen; the ground had turf on it still; it was only speckled
with shell-holes, not disembowelled or flayed. The
war had put on a sort of benignity, coming out
gallantly on the top of the earth and moving about in
the air and the sun; the warm heath, with so few dead
upon it, looked almost clement and kind, almost gay
after the scabrous mud wastes and the stink of the
captured dug-outs of the Salient, piled up to ground-
level with corpses, some feet uppermost, some heads,
like fish in a basket, making you think what wonderful
numbers there are of mankind. For a moment, the
object of all dream and desire seemed to have come;
the flaming sword was gone, and the gate of the garden
open.

Too late, as you know. We awoke from delight,
and remembered. Four years ago, three years ago,
even two years ago, a lasting repose of beatitude might
have come with that regaining of paradise! Now! The
control of our armies, jealously hugged for so long
and used, on the whole, to so little purpose, had passed
from us, thrown up in a moment of failure, dissension
and dread. While still outnumbered by the enemy we

had not won; only under a foreign Commander-
in-Chief, and with America's inexhaustible numbers
crowding behind to hold up our old arms, had our
just cause begun to prevail. And now the marred
triumph would leave us jaded and disillusioned, divided, half bankrupt; sneerers at lofty endeavour, and
yet not the men for the plodding of busy and orderly
peace; bilious with faiths and enthusiasms gone sour
in the stomach. That very night I was to hear the old
Australian sneer again. The British corps on their left,
at work in the twisty valley and knucklesome banks
of the Somme, had failed to get on quite as fast as
they and the Canadian troops on their right. "The
Canadians were all right, of course, but the Tommies!
Well, we might have known!" They had got rid, they
chucklingly said, of their own last "Tommy officers"
now; they wanted to have it quite clear that in
England's war record they were not involved except
as our saviours from our sorry selves.

C. E. Montague, *Disenchantment* (1922),
pp.174–7.

There was much more excitement at home. Conan Doyle
spoke for many in his delight that peace moves, German
diplomacy, political intrigues and civilian defeatism now all
seemed over.

Haig is moving!
Three plain words are all that matter,
Mid the gossip and the chatter,
Hopes in speeches, fears in papers,
Pessimistic froth and vapours –
Haig is moving!

Haig is moving!
We can turn from German scheming,
From humanitarian dreaming,

From assertions, contradictions,
Twisted facts and solemn fictions –
Haig is moving!

A. Conan Doyle, 'Haig is Moving / August 1918',
The Guards Came Through (1919), st. i–ii.

It was not only Haig who was moving. In September the Salonika force advanced after years of inactivity, and in the Middle East the British captured Damascus.

Doyle was mistaken in his hope that the arguments were over. Once it became clear that Germany was not going to recover, the prolongation of the fighting came into question. Why go on fighting unless the Allies really were bent on 'aggression and conquest'? Orders had to be issued forbidding 'peace talk'. The politicians' answer was that they and the diplomats needed time to get satisfactory peace terms. The French Premier, Clemenceau, known as 'the Tiger', told the applauding Senate in Paris why the war had to go on.

All are worthy of victory, because they will know how to honour it. Yet, however, in the ancient spot where sit the fathers of the Republic we should be untrue to ourselves if we forget that the greatest glory will be to those splendid *poilus* [common soldiers] who will see confirmed by history the titles of nobility which they themselves have earned. At the present moment they ask for nothing more than to be allowed to complete the great work which will assure them of immortality. What do they want and what do you? To keep on fighting victoriously until the moment when the enemy will understand there is no possible negotiation between crime and right.

Georges Clemenceau, as reported in *The Times*,
19 September 1918.

Owen, who was once again in France, read this inelegant translation and wrote a satirical response.

Head to limp head, the sunk-eyed wounded scanned
Yesterday's *Mail*; the casualties (typed small)
And (large) Vast Booty from our Latest Haul.
Also, they read of Cheap Homes, not yet planned,
'For', said the paper, 'when this war is done
The men's first instincts will be making homes.
Meanwhile their foremost need is aerodromes,
It being certain war has but begun.
Peace would do wrong to our undying dead, –
The sons we offered might regret they died
If we got nothing lasting in their stead.
We must be solidly indemnified.
Though all be worthy Victory which all bought,
We rulers sitting in this ancient spot
Would wrong our very selves if we forgot
The greatest glory will be theirs who fought,
Who kept this nation in integrity.'
Nation? – The half-limbed readers did not chafe
But smiled at one another curiously
Like secret men who know their secret safe.
(This is the thing they know and never speak,
That England one by one had fled to France,
Not many elsewhere now, save under France.)
Pictures of these broad smiles appear each week,
And people in whose voice real feeling rings
Say: How they smile! They're happy now, poor things.

> Wilfred Owen, 'Smile, Smile, Smile', *Poems*
> (1920).

This was Owen's last protest, written in the hope that it
might stir Sassoon into writing something more powerful,
but Sassoon had no more to say.

Opposition to the war was still very limited. Ever since
March anti-German feeling had been growing, bringing a
revival in the campaign against spies and aliens. There was
excitement in June over allegations that the German secret
service had compiled a Black Book listing 47 000 public
figures in Britain whose personal lives or opinions made them
vulnerable to blackmail. In August a petition was delivered

in London. Calling for the internment of all foreigners still at large and the eradication of German influence in Government circles, it was supported by two miles of signatures and a procession which included representative trade unionists, businessmen and British and Colonial soldiers. October brought the Central Powers' formal request for peace, the collapse of Turkey, mutinies in the German fleet and Allied success in Italy, but *John Bull* was unwavering in its demands. Under the heading of 'PEOPLE versus POLITICIANS / DESTROY THE BEAST – HAND OVER THE KAISER – FOR THE HANGMAN', Bottomley took up his usual role as spokesman for 'the people' in general and 'Tommy and Jack' in particular.

> Let us cease to talk of war. Whilst Foch and Haig and Pershing are putting the finishing touches to the operations in the field – and Beatty is 'standing by', ready for any emergency, on sea – let us talk of Peace. In other words, what are our terms for allowing Germany, in any form, to remain on the map of Europe? That is the only question now to be settled, and we, the People of Britain, will settle it for ourselves, so far as our own interests are concerned – leaving it to the democracies of our Allies to adopt a similar course. But we haven't a moment to spare. Unless we are alert, we shall find that whilst our dearest and best are falling in their thousands in these last days of the war, the gentlemen in the black coats [politicians] are taking the credit for their glorious deeds, and have gone behind our backs and bartered away the blood of our heroes. 'We have no quarrel with the German people' – they will declare – 'our quarrel is with the system'. And they will let the blonde brutes of Middle Europe loose upon the world once more, to procreate their lustful and bloody breed and pollute the human race with their lewd, coarse and savage strain. The People's Mandate is – Destroy the Beast! And that is the purpose of my present campaign. 'We do not desire the Unconditional Surrender of the German people,' said Mr Churchill the other day. Don't we! For all

practical purposes, the German people are the German Army – take that away and only the women and children, and a few old men, are left. But, all the same, we will begin with the Kaiser. . . .

'The German People', forsooth! How, when and where have they ever dissociated themselves from the Kaiser and his villainies? It is too late to pretend to do so now that they are beaten, and the game is up. And whilst they must be sentenced to redeem by the sweat of their toil the precious treasure we have poured out in this struggle for Freedom and Right, their War Lords must pay with their heads for the blood *we* have lost. That, and that only, is the way to end war for all time. Be weak and hesitating now – listen to slobbery sentimentality about mercy and forgiveness – and as sure as Heaven is above us, you will have another war, more terrible even than this has been, in a generation's time. Thus would you be an accessory before the fact to the slaughter and torture and outrage of your children and their children – and the curse of Cain would be upon you. *That* is what I want the People of this country to realise. Before the bells ring out their peals of joy, let them toll for the lost souls – rendered up to the Devil by the stern decree of a righteous God – of the murderers of our sons and brothers, husbands and fathers. Remember what we risked – our Empire, our country, our homes, our liberties, our lives, our all – to rid the world of this monster – who had stalked the earth for forty years, seeking whom he might devour. And now that we have him by the throat, shall we allow him to escape?

Horatio Bottomley, *John Bull*, 26 October 1918.

That statement of war aims should be compared with those by Lloyd George and Wells at the beginning of this chapter. Events were to show that Bottomley's claim to represent public opinion was unpleasantly near the truth.

On 2 November a mass meeting in the Albert Hall demanded unconditional German surrender with no peace negotiations. Austria capitulated on the 3rd. Wilfred Owen, who had won the Military Cross in October by turning a captured machine-gun on the enemy, was killed by another machine-gun on 4 November. The Armistice was signed on the 11th, and the guns stopped firing at 11 a.m.

In a debate which still continues, some commentators in 1918 and later blamed the newspapers and politicians for prolonging the war. Others argued that the Armistice had come too soon, because it left Germany still united and uninvaded: it might have been better for everybody in the long term if the German people had been immediately faced with the fact of defeat. The Kaiser had managed to escape to Holland, but the President who replaced him assured the returning troops that they were unconquered. In the short term, however, the Allied Governments certainly used the time to obtain enormous concessions under the Armistice with a detailed Peace Treaty still to come. In return for Allied promises about peace terms Germany agreed to evacuate all captured territory within two weeks, hand over colonies, surrender all prisoners and an immense number of guns, planes, vehicles and ships, and cancel the treaties she had imposed on the countries she had defeated. The Allies temporarily occupied the left bank of the Rhine, retained their prisoners and continued the blockade. Many of the aims of 1914 were quickly achieved. France regained the provinces she had lost to Prussia in 1870, the Kaiser had abdicated, Belgium was free, and the German military machine was dismantled. There was a chance, as so many writers and volunteers had hoped, that out of the wreckage of the old world a new and better one might be constructed.

7 Peace to End Peace

After the Armistice

So at last the dark cloud of war, which had seemed so endless and so impenetrable as it covered the whole heavens from the Eastern horizon to the Western, passed and drifted beyond us, while a dim sun in a cold sky was the first herald of better times. Laden with debt, heart-heavy for its lost ones, with every home shaken and every industry dislocated, its hospitals filled with broken men, its hoarded capital all wasted upon useless engines – such was the world which the accursed German Kultur had left behind it. Here was the crop reaped from those navy bills and army estimates, those frantic professors and wild journalists, those heavy-necked, sword-trailing generals, those obsequious, arrogant courtiers, and the vain, swollen creature whom they courted. Peace had come at last – if such a name can be given to a state where international bitterness will long continue, and where within each frontier the bulk of mankind, shaken by these great events from the ruts of custom, contend fiercely for some selfish advantage out of the general chaos. In the East, Russia, like some horrible invertebrate creature, entangles itself with its own tentacles, and wrestles against itself with such intricate convulsions that one can hardly say which attacks or which defends, which is living or which already dead. But the world swings on the divine cycle. He who made the planet from the fire-mist is still at work moulding with set and sustained purpose the destinies of a universe which at every stage can only reach the higher through its combat with the lower.

Here the historian's task is done. It has occupied

and alleviated many heavy days. . . . He lays down his pen at last with the deep conviction that the final results of this great convulsion are meant to be spiritual rather than material, and that upon an enlightened recognition of this depends the future history of mankind. Not to change rival frontiers, but to mould the hearts and spirits of men – there lie the explanation and the justification of all that we have endured. The system which left seven million people dead upon the fields of Europe must be rotten to the core. Time will elapse before the true message is mastered, but when that day arrives the war of 1914 may be regarded as the end of the dark ages and the start of that upward path which leads away from personal or national selfishness towards the City Beautiful upon the distant hills.

> A. Conan Doyle, *The British Campaign in France and Flanders: July to November 1918* (1919), pp.304–5.

Thus Conan Doyle ended his six-volume history of the Western Front. His fine prose already belonged to another age. He was an 'old man', a Victorian, believing in duty, work, the educative value of suffering, the reality of evil, and the ultimate goodness of the Creator. God was not dead for him. He viewed with satisfaction the destruction of German power; now 'the Frenchman may look east without a tremor, and the mists of the North Sea can cloud no menace for our islands'. Doyle feared, though, that the Peace Treaty was 'hasty and ill-considered' and that further conflict could yet emerge from competing nationalisms and the strange new phenomenon of Bolshevism. The Allies would have to stand firm.

Despite his religion, Doyle makes no mention of mercy or reconciliation; as Bottomley had hoped, such topics were not to the fore in the clamour which followed the Armistice. Lloyd George had been arguing for a 'just' peace that would not cripple the enemy: Germany should pay 'reparations' for damage to Allied civilian life but not 'indemnities' to cover military costs. However, as the Liberal leader of a largely Conservative Coalition, he depended for his power on electoral support. Only three days after the Armistice, he announced a General Election, taking advantage of his popularity as the apparent winner of the war. The electorate, now including women, was more than double its pre-war size but inexperienced and over-excited. With the Northcliffe and Bottomley papers campaigning under slogans such as 'Hang the Kaiser' and 'Make Germany Pay', Lloyd George soon found he had to change his tune. According to John Maynard Keynes, his manifesto eventually contained six points.

1. Trial of the Kaiser.
2. Punishment of those responsible for atrocities.
3. Fullest Indemnities from Germany.
4. Britain for the British, socially and industrially.
5. Rehabilitation of those broken in the war.
6. A happier country for all.

> J. M. Keynes, *The Economic Consequences of the Peace* (1919), p.131.

Keynes added, 'Here is food for the cynic. To this concoction of greed and sentiment, prejudice and deception, three weeks of the platform had reduced the powerful governors of England, who but a little while before had spoken not ignobly of Disarmament and a League of Nations and of a just and lasting peace which should establish the foundations of a new Europe.' Most of Lloyd George's promises were nonsense. With the Dutch refusing to hand over the Kaiser, there would be no war trials. Germany could not possibly pay full indemnities. The fourth point, which would now be called 'racist', was a gesture towards the contemporary British obsession that the country was under German–Jewish financial influence. The electorate was delighted, voting in the Coalition with a huge majority. Labour formed the Opposition for the first time, but the rump of the old Liberal Party, still led by Asquith, won a mere 28 seats, a defeat from which it was never to recover. Lloyd George, still a Liberal at heart, was trapped within a Tory-dominated administration and

Commons. Someone, probably Stanley Baldwin, remarked to Keynes that the new MPs were 'hard-faced men' who seemed to have made fortunes out of the war. One of them was Bottomley.

Some extreme expressions of the hate and suspicion which survived into 1919 and beyond can be found in the verse of Gilbert Frankau, who had lost a brother in the war and had fought in the trenches. In a 1919 verse letter to his sister, who had urged him to obey Christ's command to forgive the enemy, Frankau warned against German and 'red' treachery at home and recalled that Germany still regarded her grey-uniformed troops as undefeated.

> Beware lest, in your innocence you fall
> A prey to those who wish our Country ill,
> The secret enemies within her gates!

> These prate of 'peace,' 'the brotherhood of man,'
> And 'reconciliation of the world';
> These dirty hounds who, while we fought for them,
> Had gladly dragged our Empire in the dust.
> Who won the peace of which they prate? Not they:
> But simple men inspired to godlike deeds
> By love of country! . . . Men they label now
> 'Northcliffians,' 'Jingoes,' 'Kiplingites,' – these rats
> Our bodies saved from Prussian slavery. . . .

> Sister, 'tis easy thus to sneer at men
> Who loved their country better than their life:
> But did *they* save the world – your red macaws
> Who squawked in parrot-cages at the Hague?
> You say: 'Because these eyes have looked on War' –
> Who made this war, I ask you. Was it We? –
> And seen that naked horror which war is:
> That I should put aside my righteous hate,
> Lest – from that hatred – War be born again.
> I answer: 'Earth shall know enduring Peace
> So long as We, the English-speaking Folk,
> Keep bright against the Beast that sword of God
> Whose brand is graven, 'Anglo-Saxondom.' . . .'

Sister, doth Christ approve? Who knows His mind?
I would not arrogate to my poor self
The certain judgments of Divinity.
Yet if He be that Christ who said 'Repent!'
Methinks He will not punish overmuch
One who has voiced this hatred, which We feel
For those who crucified our million dead—
Aye! and our million maimed and living men. . . .

For these have not repented. Still they boast
Of their 'unbeaten field-grays.' Still they lie,
And plot with gold, and plot with cunning words
To void the justice which Our Dead demand. . . .

Gilbert Frankau, 'The Answer' (dated 26
February 1919), *Poetical Works* (1923), vol.2.

While Frankau was writing that, representatives of the victorious governments were discussing the shape of the Peace Treaty in Paris.

The Peace Conference

Paris was not a happy choice as a meeting-place. France had suffered more than the other Allies. Clemenceau was an 'old man', convinced that the struggle between France and Germany was without ending. Believing only in France, his aim was to break the enemy's power and keep it broken. Lloyd George was less pessimistic, more unscrupulous and more ready to compromise. Despite his promises to make Germany pay, he knew that British trade would not be helped by German poverty. The third of the 'Big Three', President Wilson, was seen as the great hope for a lasting peace. Under his leadership the USA had remained as aloof as possible from Europe, entering the war only as an 'Associated Power', not as an Ally. The German request for an Armistice had been sent to him alone, not to the Allied leaders. With enormous financial, military and moral superiority over the Allies and apparently with no imperialist aims, he seemed able to dictate the peace terms, but it soon emerged that his idealism was not based on international realities. He succeeded in getting agreement to a League of Nations, but he was worked round to accepting a Treaty much nearer Clemenceau's wishes than his own. His advisers, many members of the British delegation, and even Lloyd George and the British Cabinet, were appalled. Lord Milner remarked that this was 'the Peace to end peace'. The German representatives were not allowed to negotiate but only to express their objections, which they did in an exasperatingly haughty manner and to no great effect. The Treaty of Versailles was signed on 28 June 1919.

The Treaty has had its defenders as well as its critics. The politicians had been faced with an immense range of problems. They had been besieged with conflicting demands by many of the world's countries. Decisions had to be made quickly. The whole of central Europe was on the edge of economic and social breakdown. More than seven million men had been killed in the war. Revolutionary Bolshevism was spreading rapidly. Under the circumstances, some historians say, the politicians did the best they could. New countries were established, boundaries were redrawn, old claims were settled. The general disappointment at Wilson was not altogether fair; he was ill, outnumbered, under pressure from Congress and mercilessly caricatured by his opponents. His acceptance of the Treaty rested on his hope that the League of Nations would complete the task of establishing world peace (unfortunately his own Congress undermined the League from the start by refusing to allow the United States to join it). Nevertheless, on the crucial question of Germany's future, the Treaty was widely believed to be a failure. German protests centred on the 'war-guilt clause', Article 231, under which Germany accepted responsibility for loss and damage. No figure was stated, but a powerful Reparations Commission was set up to extract payment. Despite promises before the Armistice of 'equality of trade conditions', 'no punitive damages', and self-determination for colonies, German shipping and overseas possessions were taken over and huge tributes were imposed on German home industries. Moreover, Article 231 meant that Germany accepted not only financial but also moral responsibility for the war. The new Republic promptly began an enquiry into the origins of the conflict; if Germany could be shown to be not guilty, the Treaty would be revealed as unjust and not morally binding. From the French point of view, on the other hand, the Treaty set no limits to Germany's liability; if payments were not made, France could extract them by force. All this had ominous implications for the future.

The most influential British criticism came from Keynes, who attended the conference as an economic adviser but then resigned his Treasury post in order to publish his opinion of the Treaty. Keynes belonged to the 'Bloomsbury group', and the spirit and methods of Bloomsbury are evident in his book. He quotes from *The Dynasts* in his introduction, suggesting that the Immanent Will (see above, p.5) had controlled the conference; then, before developing his technical argument, he gives character portraits of Clemenceau and Wilson. The 'collapse of the President' had been 'one of the decisive moral events of history'. Wilson had been believed in as a man of authority, intellect and imagination.

> The first impression of Mr. Wilson at close quarters was to impair some but not all of these illusions. His head and features were finely cut and exactly like his photographs, and the muscles of his neck and the carriage of his head were distinguished. But, like Odysseus [who had short legs], the President looked wiser when he was seated; and his hands, though capable and fairly strong, were wanting in sensitiveness and finesse. The first glance at the President suggested not only that, whatever else he might be, his temperament was not primarily that of the student or the scholar, but that he had not much even of that culture of the world which marks M. Clemenceau and Mr. Balfour [Foreign Secretary] as exquisitely cultivated gentlemen of their class and generation. But more serious than this, he was not only insensitive to his surroundings in the external sense, he was not sensitive to his environment at all. What chance could such a man have against Mr. Lloyd George's unerring, almost medium-like, sensibility to every one immediately

round him? To see the British Prime Minister watching the company, with six or seven senses not available to ordinary men, judging character, motive, and sub-conscious impulse, perceiving what each was thinking and even what each was going to say next, and compounding with telepathic instinct the argument or appeal best suited to the vanity, weakness, or self-interest of his immediate auditor, was to realise that the poor President would be playing blind man's buff in that party. Never could a man have stepped into the parlour a more perfect and predestined victim to the finished accomplishments of the Prime Minister. The Old World was tough in wickedness anyhow; the Old World's heart of stone might blunt the sharpest blade of the bravest knight-errant. But this blind and deaf Don Quixote was entering a cavern where the swift and glittering blade was in the hands of the adversary.

But if the President was not the philosopher-king, what was he? After all he was a man who had spent much of his life at a University. He was by no means a business man or an ordinary party politician, but a man of force, personality, and importance. What, then, was his temperament?

The clue once found was illuminating. The President was like a Nonconformist minister, perhaps a Presbyterian. His thought and his temperament were essentially theological not intellectual, with all the strength and the weakness of that manner of thought, feeling, and expression. It is a type of which there are not now in England and Scotland such magnificent specimens as formerly; but this description, nevertheless, will give the ordinary Englishman the distinctest impression of the President.

J. M. Keynes, *The Economic Consequences of the Peace* (1919), pp.37–8.

This reduction of Wilson to a slow-witted preacher is not unlike the satirical portraits by Keynes's friend, Lytton

Strachey, in *Eminent Victorians* (1918), a book which signalled
the triumph of Bloomsbury's 'modern' thinking over 'old
men' and everything Victorian. Keynes helped to set the
terms of reference for the British liberal conscience for the
next twenty years or more, turning its attention away from
German guilt towards guilt at home. Plagued with remorse
at a Treaty which seemed neither just nor practicable and at
the economic and social chaos which that Treaty helped to
cause in Germany, the new generation allowed the watch on
the Rhine to lapse and eventually tolerated or in some cases
even welcomed the rise of Hitler.

Other literary men at the Paris conference included T. E.
Lawrence, who pressed in vain for Arab freedom. The Middle
East was divided up between Britain and France. Lawrence,
too, left Paris with a tormented conscience, as he recorded
in his memoirs (first published in 1935, but without the
'Introductory Chapter' from which this extract comes).

> In these pages the history is not of the Arab
> movement, but of me in it. It is a narrative of daily
> life, mean happenings, little people. Here are no lessons
> for the world, no disclosures to shock peoples. It is
> filled with trivial things, partly that no one mistake
> for history the bones from which some day a man may
> make history, and partly for the pleasure it gave me
> to recall the fellowship of the revolt. We were fond
> together, because of the sweep of the open places, the
> taste of wide winds, the sunlight, and the hopes in
> which we worked. The morning freshness of the
> world-to-be intoxicated us. We were wrought up with
> ideas inexpressible and vaporous, but to be fought for.
> We lived many lives in those whirling campaigns,
> never sparing ourselves: yet when we achieved and the
> new world dawned, the old men came out again and
> took our victory to re-make in the likeness of the
> former world they knew. Youth could win, but had
> not learned to keep: and was pitiably weak against
> age. We stammered that we had worked for a new
> heaven and a new earth, and they thanked us kindly
> and made their peace.

All men dream: but not equally. Those who dream by night in the dusty recesses of their minds wake in the day to find that it was vanity: but the dreamers of the day are dangerous men, for they may act their dream with open eyes, to make it possible. This I did. I meant to make a new nation, to restore a lost influence, to give twenty millions of Semites the foundations on which to build an inspired dream-palace of their national thoughts. So high an aim called out the inherent nobility of their minds, and made them play a generous part in events: but when we won, it was charged against me that the British petrol royalties in Mesopotamia were become dubious, and French Colonial policy ruined in the Levant.

I am afraid that I hope so. We pay for these things too much in honour and in innocent lives. I went up the Tigris with one hundred Devon Territorials, young, clean, delightful fellows, full of the power of happiness and of making women and children glad. By them one saw vividly how great it was to be their kin, and English. And we were casting them by thousands into the fire to the worst of deaths, not to win the war but that the corn and rice and oil of Mesopotamia might be ours. The only need was to defeat our enemies (Turkey among them), and this was at last done in the wisdom of Allenby with less than four hundred killed, by turning to our uses the hands of the oppressed in Turkey. I am proudest of my thirty fights in that I did not have any of our own blood shed. All our subject provinces to me were not worth one dead Englishman.

T. E. Lawrence, *Seven Pillars of Wisdom* (1939), pp.4–5.

Lawrence's bitterness at the forgotten expense of British lives was shared by many. The official British artist at the conference, William Orpen, was sickened by the politicians' failure to recognise that the war had been fought and won by the common soldier. Orpen's group portrait of the signatories

(Plate 3) shows pompous little old men, each isolated from the others and all overwhelmed by the vainglorious grandeur of Versailles. Wilson has his back half-turned to Clemenceau, who sits in the centre next to cunning Lloyd George; in front of them the cowed German representatives, their pallor a reminder that Germany was starving as a result of the long blockade, sign a treaty which their fellow countrymen were never going to accept. Another dismayed observer in Paris was C. E. Montague, whose subsequent book, *Disenchantment* (1922), captured the general mood of the years immediately after victory (his description of the 1918 triumph has been quoted above, pp.174–6). The men who returned from military service to what Lloyd George had hoped would be 'a fit country for heroes to live in' found that the nation seemed to have little to offer but unemployment and poverty, showing no gratitude to either the dead or the survivors.

> We thought when we sat in the soup, old man, with
>   the curling flames all round,
> We thought if we didn't get scorched or choked or
>   buried or boiled or drowned,
> We thought to the end of our days on earth we should
>   live like kings uncrowned.
>
> We thought if we ever came home alive they would
>   fall on our necks half mad,
> And turn their hearts for us inside out and load us
>   with all they had;
> That nothing would be too good for us, since nothing
>   was then too bad.
>
> We thought, and the thought of it warmed us up, and
>   gave us strength anew,
> And carried us on till the task was done; we thought –
>   but it wasn't true,
> For it isn't much cop down here, old man; how is it
>   up there with you?

> George Willis, 'Two Years After', *A Ballad of
> Four Brothers* (1921).

'War Books'

Remarkably little was published about the realities of front-line fighting for nearly a decade after the Armistice. Politicians and generals produced their memoirs. Novelists such as Bennett, Lawrence and Ford exposed the corruption of British society during the war years. Shaw's *Heartbreak House* (1919) portrayed upper-class England in 1916–17, when the play was written, as a house whose occupants had seemed recklessly bent on self-destruction. However, writers who had fought in the trenches were for the most part silent, perhaps from exhaustion or perhaps in a vain effort to forget. In the absence of any lead from them, English literature moved away on a new course that most of them were subsequently unable to follow. The accepted 'major authors' of the twenties – Eliot, James Joyce, Yeats, Pound, Virginia Woolf, D. H. Lawrence – had not been directly involved in the conflict. Their work contains many allusions to the war, and Eliot's *The Waste Land* (1922) is a supreme expression of the social and spiritual aridity of post-war Europe, but they had no personal experience from which to write about the horrors that had so recently ended.

The silence was scarcely broken until 1928 when memoirs and novels began appearing which described in vivid detail the ordeal soldiers had been obliged to endure. Some of these books have already been referred to: Blunden's *Undertones of War* (1928), Sassoon's three Sherston books (1928, 1930, 1936), Aldington's *Death of a Hero* (1929), Graves's *Goodbye to All That* (1929), Manning's *The Middle Parts of Fortune* (1929), and Tomlinson's *All Our Yesterdays* (1930). Sherriff's *Journey's End* had enormously successful runs in London and New York in 1929. These works came as a revelation to people whose knowledge of the trenches had been derived from newspapers. *Journey's End* was angrily condemned because it portrayed a drunkard and a coward among front-line officers. *Goodbye to All That*, which has proved to be one of the most enduringly influential war autobiographies, was disliked even by Graves's fellow soldiers, including Sassoon and Blunden; its gossipy cynicism and its highly unreliable treatment of facts were much resented. (It has to be said that such memoirs, written years afterwards, are not the accurate records of wartime events and opinions that they have often been assumed to be; as modern researchers are at last beginning to reveal, the post-war work of a Graves, a Vera Brittain or even a Sassoon is not always consistent with the same author's wartime writings.)

One of the sharpest of many attacks on the new 'war books' came from the Right-wing essayist and ex-soldier, Douglas Jerrold, who protested that Graves and the others had made a fundamental mistake in writing from an exclusively individual viewpoint; immense historical movements could not possibly make sense in terms of one man's experience. The war had been neither meaningless nor a mere blunder, but a tragic event, both inevitable and significant. Jerrold protested that the effect of the new books was to make suffering and horror more important than the principles for which the war had been fought.

> The object, conscious or unconscious, of all these books is to simplify and sentimentalise the problem of war and peace until the problem disappears in a silly gesture of complacent moral superiority, and the four years of war are shown idiotically as four years of disastrous, sanguinary and futile battles in which everything was lost and nothing gained, a struggle begun for no purpose and continued for no reason. To present this view of war in pages of vivid and poignant prose is to create in the minds of the public a love of peace foolishly based on a barren fear of useless suffering. If the growing generation get this picture of war into their heads, it will go hardly with them indeed.
>
> If they conceive the generation of 1914 as a generation of callous and futile fools playing with fire, and of war as a mere instrument of policy carelessly applied and found, to the chagrin of the combatants, to be a very dangerous instrument, they will never learn the real lesson of the disaster. Confident that they and their contemporaries in other lands have, thanks to their eloquence and their awakened consciences, now

finally realised that men are killed and bodies maimed in war, they will go ahead, as they are doing to-day, with their policies of reconstruction, evolution and what-not, of building a new world without regard to the preferences of the inhabitants of the world as it is – the error of every militarist from the days of Alexander downwards – and they will find themselves faced, as we were faced in 1914, with what General Smuts calls 'intolerable situations' in consequence of their policies. Only if the generation now growing up in Europe and America can all, and all at once, be taught to realise that the war of 1914 was, in 1914, inevitable, will they learn not to ride their silly hobby horses so that another war will be equally inevitable. For no races of men which hold the Christian faith and are born of woman will ever grow up in the belief that principles which they have come to hold for conscience sake are to be abandoned for safety's sake. The appeal to sentiment will inevitably fail.

Douglas Jerrold, *The Lie About the War* (1930), pp.46–8.

Jerrold's argument would have been widely accepted by the older generation – comparable objections were made to Owen's poetry by Newbolt and Yeats – but the image of the war which has prevailed since 1930 has been that of the books which he attacked. Although few people today can give a coherent account of how and why the First World War began, the general opinion tends to be that it was an avoidable mistake, a futile waste and a crime; the young men were slaughtered like cattle and then the old men divided up the spoils, thereby laying the foundations for another war. Sassoon, perhaps more than any other writer, has been regarded as the spokesman for this point of view; looking at the British memorial built to replace the old town gate of Ypres on the once-deadly Menin Road (Plates 4 and 5), he saw it as a monument to hypocrisy and deceit.

Who will remember, passing through this Gate,
The unheroic Dead who fed the guns?
Who shall absolve the foulness of their fate, –
Those doomed, conscripted, unvictorious ones?
Crudely renewed, the Salient holds its own.
Paid are its dim defenders by this pomp;
Paid, with a pile of peace-complacent stone,
The armies who endured that sullen swamp.

Here was the world's worst wound. And here with
   pride
'Their name liveth for ever,' the Gateway claims.
Was ever an immolation so belied
As these intolerably nameless names?
Well might the Dead who struggled in the slime
Rise and deride this sepulchre of crime.

> Siegfried Sassoon, 'On Passing the New Menin
> Gate', *The Heart's Journey* (1928).

When Herbert Read looked back on his experiences long
afterwards, he concluded that the only result of the war for
his generation had been exhaustion, but he allowed for a more
positive attitude in his *The End of a War*. This long poem,
based on a gruesome incident on the last day of the fighting,
is in three parts: a monologue by a dying German officer
who has betrayed the advancing British into an ambush and
been killed in revenge; a dialogue between the soul and body
of a French girl raped and murdered by the Germans; and a
meditation next day by the officer in charge of the British
troops. Each of the three characters presents different ideas;
the German is still patriotic and heroic in his sentiments, the
girl is like the garden of France destroyed by the war, and
the Englishman, muddled and shaken though he is, ends his
thoughts in the belief that possibly 'we act / God's purpose
in an obscure way'.

When first this fury caught us, then
I vowed devotion to the rights of men
would fight for peace once it came again

from this unwilled war pass gallantly
to wars of will and justice.
That was before I had faced death
day in day out, before hope had sunk
to a little pool of bitterness.
Now I see, either the world is mechanic force
and this the last tragic act, portending
endless hate and blind reversion
back to the tents and healthy lusts
of animal men: or we act
God's purpose in an obscure way.
Evil can only to the Reason stand
in scheme or scope beyond the human mind.
God seeks the perfect man, planned
to love him as a friend: our savage fate
a fire to burn our dross
to temper us to finer stock
man emerging in some inconceivèd span
as something more than remnant of a dream.

To that end worship God, join the voices
heard by these waking ears. God is love:
in his will the meek heart rejoices
doubting till the final grace a dove
from Heaven descends and wakes the mind
in light above the light of human kind
in light celestial
infinite and still
eternal
bright

Herbert Read, 'Meditation of the Waking English
    Officer', *The End of a War* (1933), pp.28–9.

Chronological Table

Before the War

Date	Contemporary events	Literary events
1870–1	Franco-Prussian war ends in French defeat and loss of Alsace-Lorraine; King of Prussia proclaimed Kaiser of the new German Empire	
1888	Accession of Kaiser Wilhelm II	
1901	Accession of Edward VII	
1904	Franco-British *Entente Cordiale*	
1906	Liberals win election landslide	
1907	Plans made for Regular Army in UK to be sent as BEF to France in event of German invasion of Belgium; Territorial Army founded; second Hague Peace Conference	
1908	Asquith PM	Hardy, *The Dynasts* (1903–08); Forster, *A Room with a View*
1909	Lloyd George's 'People's Budget'; Secret Service founded	Doughty, *The Cliffs*; Angell, *The Great Illusion*
1910	Accession of George V	Forster, *Howards End*
1911	Agadir crisis; Official Secrets Act	
1912	Scott and companions die after reaching South Pole; Wilson US President	Brooke, 'Grantchester'; *Georgian Poetry 1911–1912*; Bernhardi, *Germany and the Next War*

Date	Contemporary events	Literary events

1914

	Suffragette riots; trouble in Ireland	
June	Austrian Archduke assassinated (28th)	
July	Austria declares war on Serbia (28th)	
August	Germany declares war on Russia (1st); invades Belgium, declares war on France (3rd); Britain declares war (4th); BEF to France; Kitchener begins forming New Army; Louvain burnt (25th); retreat from Mons	First recruits include Brooke, Sassoon, Sorley, Graves; Herbert Asquith, 'The Volunteer' published (8th)
September	Rheims bombarded; Germans within sight of Eiffel Tower but are halted on the Marne	Writers' Conference; declaration by 52 writers; Wells, *The War That Will End War*
October	Antwerp falls; First Ypres: BEF stops German advance; trench warfare begins; Turkey joins Central Powers	Brooke at Antwerp; Ewer, 'Five Souls'; Gibson, 'Breakfast'; Lissauer, 'Hymn of Hate'
November	Mesopotamia campaign begins; Lord Roberts dies while visiting BEF	Shaw, 'Common Sense About the War'; Thomas begins writing poetry
December	Battle of Falkland Islands ends German long-distance sea-power; Scarborough shelled; 'Christmas truce'	Lawrence, *The Prussian Officer and Other Stories*; Brooke writing '1914' sonnets

1915

March	Neuve Chapelle; severe Russian losses all year	Kipling writes 'Mary Postgate'; Lawrence finishes *The Rainbow*
April	Second Ypres; Germans use poison gas; Gallipoli landings	Brooke dies
May	*Lusitania* sunk; Zeppelin raid on London; shell shortage scandal: Kitchener criticised; Lloyd George Minister of Munitions; aliens interned	Grenfell dies

Date	*Contemporary events*	*Literary events*
July	Coal strike	James becomes British subject
October	Loos (September– November), two miles gained; Salonika landings; Nurse Cavell shot	Sorley killed; Owen and Rosenberg enlist
November	Siege of Kut	*Georgian Poetry 1913–1915*
December	Gallipoli evacuation; Haig Commander-in-Chief; war effort now to be concentrated on Western Front	
		Also published in 1915: Brooke, *1914 and Other Poems* (June); Buchan, *The Thirty-Nine Steps*; Carpenter, *The Healing of Nations*; Hueffer (later Ford), *The Good Soldier*; Gibson, *Battle*

1916

January	Conscription; Isonzo: Italians resist Austrians all year	Sorley, *Marlborough and Other Poems*
February	Verdun: French resist Germans all year	Sassoon writes 'In the Pink'
April	Kut falls; Easter Rising in Dublin	Shaw writing *Heartbreak House* (finished mid-1917); Lawrence begins *Women in Love* (finished November); Hankey, *A Student in Arms*
May–June	Jutland; Russian successes; Arab Revolt begins	Rosenberg writes 'Break of Day in the Trenches'; Gertler painting *The Merry-Go-Round*
July	'Big Push', Somme, until November: huge casualties, small gains; Lloyd George Secretary of State for War	Many writers in Somme fighting; Hodgson killed; Graves wounded
September	Lloyd George: 'The fight must be to a finish – to a knock-out'; tanks first used	Wells, *Mr Britling Sees It Through*

Date	Contemporary events	Literary events
December	Lloyd George PM with mandate to 'win the war'; German Note suggests peace negotiations	
		Also published in 1916: Bridges, ed., *The Spirit of Man*; Buchan, *Greenmantle*; Masefield, *Gallipoli*; Russell, *Justice in War-Time, Principles of Social Reconstruction*

1917

Date	Contemporary events	Literary events
January	Wilson offers to mediate	Owen and Thomas to trenches
February	Germans begin planned retreat (completed April) to 'Hindenburg Line' and step up submarine war; UK authorities secretly alarmed at risk of famine	
March	Russian revolution; Czar abdicates	
April	USA enters war as 'Associate' of Allies; Arras; French offensive fails, mutinies in French army	Thomas and West killed; Owen shellshocked; Sassoon in Hindenburg Line, then wounded
June	US troops reach front; Socialist conference in Leeds calls for British Soviets; Gothas bomb London: public outcry for revenge raids	Sassoon composes protest
July	Third Ypres ('Passchendaele'), until November; Churchill Minister of Munitions	Sassoon's protest published
August	Heavy rain all month at Ypres	Sassoon and Owen meet; Owen begins writing war poems
November	Lenin and Bolsheviks seize power in Russia; Passchendaele abandoned after 6-mile total	Graves, *Fairies and Fusiliers*; Hardy, *Moments of Vision*; *Georgian Poetry 1916–1917*

Date	Contemporary events	Literary events
	advance; 'Balfour Declaration'; Lansdowne letter	
December	Russia stops fighting; Cambrai; British take Jerusalem	
		Also published in 1917: Barbusse, *Under Fire*; Eliot, *Prufrock and Other Observations*; Gurney, *Severn and Somme*; Kipling, *A Diversity of Creatures*; Sassoon, *The Old Huntsman and Other Poems* (May); Thomas, *Poems*; Wells, *God the Invisible King* (May)

1918

Date	Contemporary events	Literary events
March	Germany imposes Treaty of Brest-Litovsk on Russia, then mounts major assault in West (21st); Allied retreat; influenza epidemic (kills millions in many countries, 1918–19)	Owen to Ripon, writes 'Strange Meeting' and other poems; Herbert Read in the retreat
April	Foch 'Co-ordinator' of Allied forces on Western Front; Haig's 'Backs to the Wall' Order	Rosenberg killed; Binyon, 'The Test'
May	Germans again nearing Paris	Sassoon sent back to France
June	Spy mania revives	Sassoon, *Counter-Attack and Other Poems*
July	Second Marne; tide turns	Sassoon wounded and sent home
August	'Black day of the German Army': Allied attack succeeds (8th); German leaders decide to seek peace; as crisis fades, strikes erupt in UK; Allies intervene in Russia	
September	Salonika advance	Owen returns to France
October	Heavy fighting; Central Powers ask Wilson for armistice; Turkey capitulates; Allies advance in Italy	

Date	Contemporary events	Literary events
November	Austria capitulates (3rd); Kaiser flees (9th); Armistice (11th); Germany disarms	Owen killed (4th)
December	Lloyd George's Coalition wins election	
		Also published in 1918: Buchan, *Mr Standfast*; Strachey, *Eminent Victorians*; Thomas, *Last Poems*; Wells, *In the Fourth Year*

After the War

1919	Treaty of Versailles (28 June): many changes to world map; agreement to establish League of Nations	*Georgian Poetry 1918–1919*; Gurney, *War's Embers*; Keynes, *The Economic Consequences of the Peace*; Kipling, *The Years Between*; Read, *Naked Warriors*; Shaw, *Heartbreak House*; Sorley, *Letters*; West, *Diary of a Dead Officer*
1920		Gibbs, *Realities of War*; Lawrence, *Women in Love*; Owen, *Poems*; Pound, *Hugh Selwyn Mauberley*; Thomas, *Collected Poems*
1922	Conservative administration under Bonar Law	Eliot, *The Waste Land*; *Georgian Poetry 1920–1922*; Joyce, *Ulysses*; Montague, *Disenchantment*; Rosenberg, *Poems*
1923	France occupies Ruhr; Baldwin PM	Frankau, *Poetical Works*; Lawrence, *Kangaroo*; Masefield, *Collected Poems*
1924	*January*: Labour administration under Ramsay MacDonald; *October*: Conservatives return under Baldwin	Ford, *Some Do Not*
1925		Ford, *No More Parades*; Read, *In Retreat*

Date	Contemporary events	Literary events
1926	General Strike	Bennett, *Lord Raingo*; Ford, *A Man Could Stand Up*. Privately printed: T. E. Lawrence, *Seven Pillars of Wisdom*
1927	Allied military control ends in Germany; Germany repudiates war guilt	
1928		Blunden, *Undertones of War*; Sassoon, *Memoirs of a Fox-Hunting Man*. First performed: Sherriff, *Journey's End*
1929	Labour returns under Mac-Donald	Aldington, *Death of a Hero*; Graves, *Goodbye to All That*. Privately printed: Manning, *The Middle Parts of Fortune*
1930	Allies leave Rhineland and Saar; Nazi gains in German elections	Arthur Bliss, *Morning Heroes* (war oratorio); Jerrold, *The Lie About the War*; Sassoon, *Memoirs of an Infantry Officer*; Tomlinson, *All Our Yesterdays*

Bibliography

The reference following each extract in the seven chapters of
this book is usually to first publication in book form but does
not necessarily indicate the source of the text quoted. The
Sources section of this Bibliography gives the editions from
which, in almost all cases, my quotations are taken. Some
other books, referred to but not quoted from, are also listed.
The version of Owen's Preface in Chapter 6 first appeared in
my *Owen the Poet* (1986), pp.146–7, and is taken directly
from his manuscript. The General section of the Bibliography
gives a few of the many books which students of the literature
and history of the Great War may find useful; most of these
books contain longer bibliographies.

Place of publication of books: London unless otherwise
stated.

Sources

Periodicals

John Bull
The Cambridge Magazine
The Daily Mail
The Daily News
The Daily Telegraph
The Labour Leader

The Nation
The Poetry Review
Punch
The Sunday Pictorial
The Times

Books

Aldington, Richard, *Death of a Hero* (1968).
Amateur Officer, An, *After Victory* (1917).
Angell, Norman, *The Great Illusion* (1911).
——, *Prussianism and its Destruction* (1914).
Asquith, H. H.: see *Through Terror to Triumph*.
Asquith, Herbert, *The Volunteer and Other Poems* (1915).

Barbusse, Henri, *Under Fire: The Story of a Squad*, tr. Fitzwater Wray (1917).

Bean, C. E. W., *Gallipoli Correspondent: The Frontline Diary of C. E. W. Bean*, ed. K. Fewster (1983).

Bernhardi, Friedrich von, *Germany and the Next War*, tr. A. H. Powles (1912).

Binyon, Laurence, *The Four Years* (1919).

Blunden, Edmund, *Poems 1914–30* (1930).

——, *Undertones of War* (1965).

Brooke, Rupert, *1914 and Other Poems* (1915).

Buxton, Charles Roden, ed., *Towards a Lasting Settlement* (1915).

Carpenter, Edward, *The Healing of Nations: And the Hidden Sources of Their Strife* (1915).

Chesterton, Cecil, *The Prussian Hath Said in His Heart –* (1914).

Churchill, Winston, *The World Crisis 1911–1918*, 2 vols (1939).

Clutton-Brock, Arthur, *Thoughts on the War* (1914).

Commager, H. S., ed., *Documents of American History* (New York: 1942).

Doughty, Charles, *The Cliffs* (1909).

Doyle, Arthur Conan, *The British Campaign in France and Flanders 1914–1918*, 6 vols (1916–20).

——, *The Guards Came Through and Other Poems* (1919).

Edmonds, J. E., comp., *History of the Great War. Based on Official Documents: Military Operations, France and Belgium*, 5 vols (1922–32).

Ewer, W. N., *Five Souls and Other War-Time Verses* (1917).

Feilding, Rowland, *War Letters to a Wife, France and Flanders, 1915–1919* (1929).

Ford, Ford Madox, *No More Parades* (1925).

Forster, E. M., *Howards End* (1969).

Frankau, Gilbert, *Poetical Works*, 2 vols (1923).

Gibbs, Philip, *Realities of War* (1920).

Gibson, W. W., *Battle* (1915).

Graves, Robert, *Goodbye to All That*, 2nd impression (1929).

Grey, Sir Edward: see *Through Terror to Triumph*.

Gurney, Ivor, *Collected Poems*, ed. P. J. Kavanagh (1982).

——, *War Letters*, ed. R. K. R. Thornton (Ashington/Manchester: 1983).

Haig, Douglas, *The Private Papers of Douglas Haig*, ed. Robert Blake (1952).

Hankey, Donald, *A Student in Arms* (1916).

Hardy, Thomas, *The Dynasts: An Epic-Drama of the War with Napoleon* (1903–08).

——, *Complete Poems* (1976).

Hodgson, W. N., *Verse and Prose in Peace and War* (1916).
Housman, A. E., *Collected Poems* (1960).
James, D., *Lord Roberts* (1954).
Jerrold, Douglas, *The Lie About the War*, Criterion Miscellany No. 9 (1930).
Jones, David, *In Parenthesis* (1937).
Keynes, John Maynard, *The Economic Consequences of the Peace* (1919).
Kipling, Rudyard, *A Diversity of Creatures* (1917).
———, *The Years Between* (1919).
Langguth, A. J., *Saki: A Life of Hector Hugh Munro* (1981).
Lawrence, D. H., *Complete Short Stories* (1968).
———, *Kangaroo* (1970).
———, *Women in Love* (1921).
Lawrence, T. E., *Seven Pillars of Wisdom: A Triumph*, 5th edition (1976).
Lloyd George, David, *War Memoirs*, New Edition, 2 vols (1938).
MacColl, D. S., *Bull, and Other War Verses* (1919).
Manning, Frederic, *The Middle Parts of Fortune* (1977).
Martin, Bernard, *Poor Bloody Infantry: A Subaltern on the Western Front 1916–1917* (1987).
Masefield, John, *Gallipoli* (1916).
Montague, C. E., *Disenchantment* (1922).
Newbolt, Henry, *Collected Poems 1897–1907* (n.d.).
Newton, W. Douglas, *War* (1914).
Nietzsche, Friedrich, *Thus Spoke Zarathustra*, tr. R. J. Hollingdale (Harmondsworth: 1972).
Nicholson, Sir Lothian, and MacMullen, H. T., *History of the East Lancashire Regiment in the Great War, 1914–1918* (1936).
Noyes, Alfred, *The Wine-Press: A Tale of War* (Edinburgh: 1913).
Owen, Wilfred, *Collected Letters*, ed. Harold Owen and John Bell (1967).
———, *Complete Poems and Fragments*, ed. Jon Stallworthy, 2 vols (1983).
Read, Herbert, *Naked Warriors* (1919).
———, *The Contrary Experience* (1963).
———, *The End of a War* (1933).
Repington, C. à Court, *The First World War 1914–1918: Personal Experiences*, 2 vols (1920).
Richards, Frank, *Old Soldiers Never Die* (1933, reissued 1983).
Roberts, Lord: see James, D.
Rosenberg, Isaac, *Collected Works*, ed. I. M. Parsons (1979).
Russell, Bertrand, *Autobiography*, 2 vols (1968).
———, *Justice in War-Time* (1916).

——, *Principles of Social Reconstruction* (1916).
Sassoon, Siegfried, *Collected Poems 1908–1956* (1961).
——, *Diaries 1915–1918*, ed. Rupert Hart-Davis (1983).
——, *The Complete Memoirs of George Sherston* (1937).
[Scott, Robert]: *Captain Scott's Message to England* (1913). See also Turley, Charles.
Shaw, George Bernard, *Heartbreak House* (1919).
——, *What I Really Wrote About the War* (1931).
Sherriff, R. C., *Journey's End: A Play in Three Acts* (1929).
Sorley, Charles Hamilton, *Marlborough and Other Poems* (1916).
Thomas, Edward, *Collected Poems*, ed. R. George Thomas (Oxford: 1978).
Through Terror to Triumph ('British Statesmen on why the War Began and How the Empire will Settle it') (Edinburgh: 1914).
Tomlinson, H. M., *All Our Yesterdays* (1930).
Turley, Charles, *The Voyages of Captain Scott* (1914).
Viereck, George Sylvester, *Songs of Armageddon* (New York: 1916).
Wells, H. G., *In the Fourth Year: Anticipations of a World Peace* (1918).
——, *Mr Britling Sees It Through* (1916).
——, *The War That Will End War* (1914).
West, Arthur Graeme, *Diary of a Dead Officer* (1919).
Willis, George, *A Ballad of Four Brothers* (1921).
Winnington Ingram, Arthur F., *A Day of God: Being Five Addresses on the Subject of the Present War* (1914).
Winter, Denis, *Death's Men: Soldiers of the Great War* (1978).
Yeats, W. B., *Collected Poems* (1950).

General

Bergonzi, Bernard, *Heroes' Twilight: A Study of the Literature of the Great War* (1965).
Clarke, I. F., *Voices Prophesying War 1763–1984* (1966).
Delany, Paul, *D. H. Lawrence's Nightmare: The Writer and His Circle in the Years of the Great War* (Hassocks: 1979).
Dunn, J. C., *The War the Infantry Knew, 1914–1919: Chronicle of Service in France and Belgium* (1938, reissued 1987).
Falls, Cyril B., *War Books: A Critical Guide* (1930).
Graham, Desmond, *The Truth of War: Owen, Blunden and Rosenberg* (Manchester: 1984).
Guinn, Paul, *British Strategy and Politics 1914 to 1918* (1965).

Haig, Douglas, *Despatches: December 1915–April 1919*, ed. J. H. Boraston (1919).
Harries, Meirion and Susie, *War Artists* (19' ' .
Hibberd, Dominic, *Owen the Poet* (1986).
——, and Onions, John, eds, *Poetry of the Great War: An Anthology* (1986).
Hueffer (later Ford), Ford Madox, *When Blood is Their Argument: An Analysis of Prussian Culture* (1915).
Keegan, John, *The Face of Battle* (1976).
Klein, Holger, ed., *The First World War in Fiction: A Collection of Critical Essays* (1976).
Laffin, John, ed., *Letters from the Front, 1914–1918* (1973).
Lentin, A., *Guilt at Versailles: Lloyd George and the Pre-history of Appeasement* (1985).
Liddell Hart, B. H., *History of the First World War* (1970).
Macdonald, Lyn, *Somme* (1983).
Marwick, Arthur, *The Deluge: British Society and the First World War* (1965).
Middlebrook, Martin, *The First Day on the Somme: 1 July 1916* (1971).
Orpen, William, *An Onlooker in France, 1917–1919* (1921).
Panichas, G., ed., *Promise of Greatness* (1968).
Robbins, Keith, *The First World War* (1984).
Roby, K. E., *A Writer at War: Arnold Bennett 1914–1918* (Baton Rouge: 1972).
Rothwell, V. H., *British War Aims and Peace Diplomacy 1914–1918* (1971).
Searle, G. R., *The Quest for National Efficiency* (Oxford: 1971).
Swartz, Marvin, *The Union of Democratic Control in British Politics during the First World War* (Oxford: 1971).
Taylor, A. J. P., *English History, 1914–1945* (1965).
Terraine, John, *To Win a War, 1918: The Year of Victory* (1978).
Vellacott, Jo, *Bertrand Russell and the Pacifists in the First World War* (Brighton: 1980).
Weintraub, Stanley, *Bernard Shaw 1914–1918: Journey to Heartbreak* (1973).

Index